Alcyon R. Fleck

Whither Thou Goest

By
Alcyon Ruth Fleck

TEACH Services, Inc.
New York

pg 12

2006 07 08 09 10 11 12 · 5 4 3 2 1

Copyright © 2006 TEACH Services, Inc.
ISBN-13: 978-1-57258-420-4
ISBN 1-57258-420-3
Library of Congress Control Number: 2006922157

Published by

TEACH Services, Inc.
www.TEACHServices.com

Dedication

In bringing this story together Ken and I have realized how much we owe our Christian parents for raising us to know and love God, and to have faith that the Seventh-day Adventist Church is God's true church for these last days. We thank God for our rich heritage. It is to the memory of these four people, Sam and Hazel Logan and James and Ida Fleck that I want to dedicate this book.

Contents

Contents

Acknowledgement

I owe a lot of credit to my husband, Ken, in the development of this story. He has given me his whole-hearted support and encouragement. He has also given me the space to spend hours and days on my computer, and then served as my private critic and editor. Actually, we have done this together as well as most other things in our lives.

Introduction

Our world today is confusing and complex. Important decisions are many times difficult. Especially, as Christians, we may wonder what God's will for our lives really is. A quotation from *Christ's Object Lessons* has been meaningful to me. **"Not more surely is the place prepared for us in the heavenly mansions than is the special place designated on earth where we are to work for God."** (COL. p 327.) I am convinced that God has a special plan for each of us.

Many times we don't understand the twists and turns our lives take, but Ken and I have learned that, if we allow him to, God does orchestrate events to not only show us His plan, but prepare us for that plan. That may take years and even difficult experiences.

I have written the saga of God's dealing in our lives to illustrate this truth that we have experienced. **God had a plan for our lives.** I firmly believe that He was directing events for Ken and me long before we even met or were old enough to understand it. There were many times in our youth when we could have gone different directions. This story illustrates how God was steering us to find each other and preparing us for things that were beyond our wildest dreams.

In my role as one of the Founders and Director of International Children's Care, I have tried to instill this truth in the hearts of the children who come to us, most of them from unbelievably hopeless situations, especially as they near the age when critical decisions are made affecting their future. Many of them would not even have lived. We give them Christian homes, love, security, education, and especially the knowledge that they have a Father in Heaven. He knows them and has a plan for them, not just in this life, but, also for eternity, and that makes all the difference.

Young people today will have meaning and purpose in their lives when they realize that God does have a plan for them. And if they allow Him to, God will bring them real fulfillment and happiness. This involves every important step in their lives, their choices of friends, of their life work, and especially their choice of a life companion. They will find that God can safely be trusted in everything.

Ken and I have experienced this and we can look back and see God leading us, even when we didn't understand or see the road ahead. As you read the story you can see that even some apparently insignificant events contributed to the preparation that we needed, and how God took two very ordinary kids from different areas and brought them together to be part of His plan. It is amazing to us to look back and realize how so many events in our lives were in that plan to prepare us for something vastly bigger than we could have dreamed up.

International Children's Care is the thrilling project that has capped our lives. Besides the exciting and fulfilling years we spent as missionaries, we have the joy of knowing that hundreds of lives have been changed. Even though we didn't plan it, God had International Children's Care in his heart all along, as you will see from the story. The ICC program, a Village Home plan, was begun when Ken retired from the ministry in 1978. It is supported entirely from private donations, and is now in 19 countries. Children from our care now include doctors, nurses, pastors, teachers, and other professionals, with God's blessing and all to His honor and glory. You can learn more of that story by reading *Child of the Crossfire* and *The Leap of Faith*.

Our lives have been blessed and enriched beyond description, and it is even more thrilling to realize that God had us in His plan possibly before we were even born. I would urge each reader to determine to allow God to develop **His Plan in Your Life.**

Chapter 1

Lone Juniper Farm

"Our new home is just over the next rise!" James announced to his young wife, Ida. "All of this land that you see on both sides is ours."

"Where are the closest neighbors?" she questioned, with a concerned look on her face.

"Well, the Opsunds live down beyond our place in the draw. They are really the closest. Of course on these big farms, the houses are pretty scattered."

Ida grew up in the Portland area, a growing town in the new West. When she married James Fleck she knew that he had a homestead in Central Oregon and that they would move there eventually. But the reality of an isolated home on the prairie had not hit her until this moment.

James' dream of developing his homestead into a wheat farm was delayed while he worked to earn enough to establish their home in Madras. During that time little Kenneth was born. By the time the baby was 18 months old, James had gone to the homestead to prepare to move his family.

At last his dreams were to be realized. He was bringing his little family home. Coming over the brow of the hill, Ida saw the lone house and windmill on the right. "Is that our place?" she asked, excitement in her voice. "Is that our house?"

1

"Yes, that's it," he answered, anxiously watching the expression on her face. "It's not fancy but it's sturdy, and it's ours." He fervently hoped she would love the prairie as he did. He realized that the house did look small against the wide expanse of the fields around it.

"I can hardly wait to see inside," she said, with as much enthusiasm as she could muster.

The livery wagon that was bringing them from the train station at Paxton, a few miles over the hills from the ranch, stopped at the gate. Their earthly belongings were on the back of the wagon, trunks, a few pieces of furniture, and supplies to last awhile.

James lifted his wife and baby down from the wagon, opened the gate and led them to the front door. The two-story house was modest but sturdy and well built. James had prepared the simple house as best he could, but he watched Ida's face as she surveyed her new domain. "It's your house, Ida. You decide where you want the furniture." He and the driver were ready to unload.

Ida took a quick look around, and then began directing the men. Soon every thing was arranged according to her directions. With all in place, Ida surveyed the effect and was satisfied. "I'll unload the boxes later, but for now we need to find the food box! Kenneth is hungry."

By then little Kenneth was demanding attention. When she finally had him fed and asleep, she went to work arranging her new home. There wasn't much to do in the parlor, the furniture had already been placed where she directed. But the kitchen boxes needed to be unpacked. By late afternoon she had found enough food for them to eat a snack.

Before retiring that night, the young couple went into their parlor. There were no curtains at the windows yet, but they did have a carpet in the living area. Already there was an atmosphere of home. James sat on one end of the couch. "Come here, Sweetheart. Let's just enjoy the feel of our home for a few minutes."

When Ida joined him, he hugged her to him. "I've been dreaming of this day for so long. You know a house isn't a home without a wife. Here we are together, and our beautiful, little first-born son is sleeping in his crib upstairs. I really feel like a family man now!"

Ida laughed. "Well, you are a family man, and I am your lucky wife. I had a dream, too. It was to marry a Christian man who really loved me, and to have children who would learn to know and love Jesus."

James drew her closer. "We aren't rich, but we have each other, and we have a healthy little boy. Now we have our own home, even if it is humble."

"It's as good as a mansion, James, where there is love and where God reigns."

"Ida, I think it would be appropriate for us to just have a special prayer, sort of a dedication for this home. What do you say?"

"Oh, James, that would be wonderful, and let's vow to raise our son, and any other children we have, for God. We don't know what plans God has for him, but I am sure He does have plans."

The one kerosene lamp on the library table cast shadows on the kneeling couple as James began to pray. "Dear Father in Heaven. We come to you tonight to thank you, and to ask for a special blessing on our new home and our family—."

When he finished Ida joined her petitions with her husband's. As they rose to their feet, James took her in his arms. "I will thank God every day for my beautiful wife, and my precious little son." Ida smiled into his eyes, blinking back the tears in her own eyes.

Life on the homestead soon settled into a routine. James was busy from morning till night, doing the fall plowing and planting. He was proud of his horses that he used to work the land. There were two cows that provided milk, and Ida was getting started raising chickens to provide their eggs. Her days were full, cooking, cleaning and caring for little Kenneth.

One evening as the sun was getting low on the horizon, James came into the kitchen where Ida was busy preparing supper. "Come with me, Ida, I want to show you something!" and he took her by the hand. "We'd better take the baby, too. I want to take you up to the top of the slope above the house."

He carried little Kenneth, and Ida gathered up her full skirt to follow him across the field, through the dry grass. Up at the top, James stopped and pointed off to the west. "Do you see that lone juniper tree off yonder at the top of the rise? It can be seen for miles from all directions. In clearing the land, we always worked around that juniper."

"It does look lonesome up there by itself," Ida observed.

James went on, "That juniper has stood through many a storm. Its trunk is sturdy and strong. We will be like that, strong against the storms of life. I would like to call our place, **The Lone Juniper Farm**. What do you say?"

"I like that, James. Really, that juniper is like you are, strong and rugged. I know I can always count on you. Yes, let's call our place, **The Lone Juniper Farm!**"

Chapter 2

Will Mama Die?

Breakfast was over. James had already gone out to the fields to work on fences, and Kenneth was playing happily in the yard with Buster. Ida was standing at the kitchen sink, finishing the dishes. *For some reason I don't feel ambitious this morning. Why am I so tired? As soon as I finish here I think I'll lie down on the couch. I'll check on Kenneth first.* The little three-year old was engrossed in a road he was making for his new little truck that Grandpa Lashier had given him.

"Don't go out of the yard, dear. Mama is lying down for a few minutes."

"I won't, Mama. Did you see what I am making? This is our house here and that rock over there is Gateway." She felt free to leave him in his play, and settled down on the couch with a sigh.

She soon drifted off into a troubled sleep. When she awoke she wondered, *what time is it? I must check on Kenneth again.* She opened the door to check on her little son, and sighed with relief that he was still busy playing. It was time to start dinner. Her head was pounding and her throat hurt, but with great effort she stoked the fire and began peeling the potatoes. By the time James opened the back door, dinner was almost ready.

"It smells good around here! Quite a change from when I was batching it!" When he came close to Ida to give her a kiss, he noticed the distressed look on her face, and then looked more closely. Her face was flushed. "What's the matter, Ida? You look sick!"

"I'm afraid I am. My head hurts so bad, and my throat hurts, too. I hope I'm not getting that terrible flu we've been hearing about."

With alarm James put his hand on her head. "Ida, you have a fever. You must go to bed."

"I guess I should, but let's eat dinner first. Call Kenneth in and I'll dish up." Ida picked at her food, but drank a lot of water.

As soon as they finished eating, James told her, "Go upstairs to bed, dear. I'll take care of things down here. Maybe a good sleep will help."

But when he checked on her later, he found that her face was hotter and she barely answered him. "My head hurts so bad, and I can hardly swallow!"

The next few days were a blur in the Fleck household. James hardly slept. Besides caring for his little son, he kept a vigil at Ida's bedside. A neighbor woman, known as the community nurse, came to help him. She kept bathing the sick young woman with cold towels to try to bring the fever down, but Ida tossed in delirium.

Little Kenneth was lost and confused without his mother. "What's wrong with Mama?" he kept asking his father.

"Mama is very sick, son. You must be quiet and good." The little fellow kept wanting to go to his mother, but they kept him out. They didn't want him to be exposed to the dreaded flu. The neighbor woman spent all the time she could helping James care for Ida, but she couldn't be there night and day. James felt so frightened and alone. He continued the home remedies that the woman was using, but they did little good. He began to despair for her life. He knew that hundreds of people were dying from this dreaded malady.

One evening, while the neighbor was with Ida, James was caring for Kenneth. They had a lonely meal together, and then he took his son to the parlor and, sitting on the sofa, pulled him onto his lap.

"Is Mama going to die?" Fear was in his eyes as he asked the dreaded question.

"I hope not, son, but we need to keep on praying that Jesus will make her well."

"Does Jesus hear us for sure?" the boy asked.

"Jesus hears us for sure," his father assured him. "He knows what is best for us all the time."

"Let's pray again. I want Jesus to know how much I need Mama." James eyes filled with tears, and he thought, *I want him to know how much I need her, too. O Lord, please hear our prayer. Give me more faith. I can't think of losing Ida.*

"Yes, son, let's pray again. You can pray first, and then I will pray." And the father and son knelt down there in that lonesome house on the prairie, the kerosene lamp on the table giving the only light.

Kenneth began to pray in his childish way and with his childish faith. "Dear Jesus, can you hear us? Please listen. My mama is so sick. Papa and I need her so much. Please don't let her die! Amen."

James struggled to control his voice. "Oh Lord, if there is some sin in my life, please forgive me. You are the Creator and have all power. Please hear our prayer tonight for Mama. Please give her back to us. We ask it in the name of your son, Jesus. Amen."

When they rose to their feet, James noticed that Kenneth's face had brightened. "Jesus is going to make her well. I'm sure He heard us."

Oh for the faith of a child! James said to himself. He helped Kenneth into his nightshirt and tucked him into bed. When he went to Ida's room she was asleep. Her face was still flushed and hot, but he knew his neighbor needed to go and care for her family. "You had better go home and rest. I'll take over now." And soon he was left alone with his wife, apparently delirious, and his little boy, now sleeping peacefully.

James slept fitfully in the rocker near Ida's bed. She stirred occasionally, but no longer moaned. As the sun began to lighten the eastern skies, he heard something. Rushing to Ida's side. He looked at her intently. Her eyes seemed to be partially open. Then he saw her lips moving, "Where am I?"

Could it be possible! "Ida, can you hear me?"

"Yes, but where am I?" she asked again, her voice barely audible.

"You are right here at home in your bed. You have been sick. How do you feel?"

"I don't know. My head doesn't hurt, but I'm so tired. Where's Kenneth?"

"He's right next door in his room asleep. It's early morning." James put his hand on her forehead. " I think your fever is down. Are you hungry, dear?"

"No, but I am thirsty." With that James hurried downstairs to pump some fresh water into a glass. . When he returned to her room, her eyes were more open, and he helped her lift her head for a drink of water. "My mouth was so dry," she whispered.

James stayed with her, holding her hand until she drifted off into sleep, this time a healing sleep. When he heard Kenneth at the door, he called, "Come on in, son." Then drawing him closer, he told him, "Your mama is better. I am sure that Jesus heard our prayers. But she has been so sick it will be awhile before she can get up. She's asleep now, but you can talk to her when she wakes up."

"Oh Papa! Is she really better? Jesus really can hear us, can't He?"

James had been surprised at his son's comprehension of the crisis, but he had been talking well for a long time. He and Ida had often told each other, "We have a very bright, intelligent little son." But James would add, "That may make it all the more complicated to raise him in the fear of God. Sometimes he seems too wise for his own good!"

Later that morning, Ida asked for something to eat. The helpful neighbor came by expecting to take her turn at the bedside, or, perish the thought, find she had passed away during the night. "I can't believe this," she told James. "She must have passed the crisis in the night."

"Yes, I think she did. God is so good."

"Well, you won't need me to stay today, but I'll get her a little gruel and fix breakfast for you and the boy before I go."

"I'll appreciate that." James told her how thankful he was for her help during those horrible days.

Later, Ida seemed to rally and ate a little of the gruel. "I think there is a little boy waiting to see you," James told her.

"Please bring him to me. How long have I been sick?"

"It's been several days, Ida, and Kenneth has been asking for you, but we couldn't let him in, because this flu is contagious. I think it is safe now, your fever seems to be gone."

When Kenneth went to his mother's room he tiptoed in, but when he saw that she was awake and smiling a little, he hurried over and put his hand on her arm. "Mama! We were so scared about you! I was afraid you would die, but you didn't. Papa and I prayed for you last night. He told me that Jesus could really hear, and he sure did!"

In the background James' eyes filled with tears. In his heart he was saying over and over again, *Thank you, Lord, Oh thank you so much. You heard my prayers, but you really honored the simple faith of our little son. I'm so thankful for what you did for us, and I learned, too, that You really do hear us when we pray.*

Chapter 3

The North Woods

Far away to the north, completely unknown to the Fleck family, a significant event was about to take place. It concerned the young Logan family.

The snow began falling in the early afternoon, covering the former blanket of several inches. Before nightfall the flakes were huge, falling thick and fast. Hazel looked out the window of the snug log cabin. *Looks like we got the cabin finished just in time. It's only the first week of November. I wonder if winter has really set in.*

Her husband, Sam, was still out doing his chores, feeding the animals and milking Brindle. Two-year-old Quentin played with his blocks on the floor.

They had purchased a piece of land ten miles up the mountain from the small town of Grand Forks, British Columbia. Their only neighbors were a colony of Doukhobors, a Russian sect, who lived communal style. They spoke little English, but seemed friendly.

The young couple built the cabin with their own hands. Sam cut the trees from their forest, then peeled and notched them. Together they hoisted the logs into place. The cabin consisted of a kitchen-living area on the first floor with a loft for sleeping.

Hazel made and hung fluffy, starched curtains at the windows. Bright, rag rugs covered the smooth, plank floors. A wood range dominated the room, furnishing heat as well as a place to cook. Their two rocking chairs could be drawn up close to the stove in cold weather. A gingham cloth covered the heavy, square oak table.

Hazel opened the cabin door. Looking out on the white, silent world, she saw that the giant flakes were now falling thicker than ever. There was anxiety on her face. She was heavy with child and knew that her time could come any day. Their only mode of transportation in the snow was a sleigh, pulled by their faithful mare, Molly. *This would be a raw night for Sam to go for the doctor,* she thought.

She turned back to the stove and the gravy she was making for the mashed potatoes. A pot of beans simmered at the back, and cornbread was in the oven. Sam would be coming in soon, cold and hungry.

Two-year-old Quentin followed her around, asking for his supper. "Just a little bit longer, Sonny. Papa will soon be in. Then we can eat."

When she heard her husband stomping the snow from his boots on the porch she began dishing up the food. A kerosene lamp on the table and another on a shelf, with a metal reflector, furnished the only light, casting shadows in the room, and the black kitchen range crackled in the corner.

"Looks like this storm is going to be a corker!" Sam exclaimed as he hung his coat on the nail by the door. "I'm glad I don't have to go anyplace tonight. I'd rather sit by my own fireside!"

"I hope you don't have to go anyplace tonight," Hazel said, warily. "I've had this uncomfortable feeling all afternoon. You know it is time."

He looked at her closely. "Are you really serious? Do you really think this could be the night?"

"Well, I wouldn't want you to make the trip all the way down the hill on a false alarm, but I do have this strange feeling."

"Let's hope this baby waits until morning to send me down the hill. However, we mustn't take any chances. Tell me as soon as you feel any real pains."

They sat down to eat, Quentin in his high chair. After thanking God for the food and for their shelter from the storm, Sam helped himself to the mashed potatoes. "It sure feels good to come into this cozy cabin and find such a good supper."

"I'm glad you and Jess finished the roof in time," his wife commented. "With our cellar full, and that great stack of wood out there, we should be taken care of this winter. I just wish the snow had waited until after this baby arrives."

"Well, Molly will have to pull the sleigh instead of the buggy, if this is the night." Her husband's face showed his concern.

Hazel cleared the dishes, filling the big granite dishpan with hot water from the steaming teakettle. A bucket of cold water stood near the door where Sam had brought it from the well. After finishing the dishes, she sat in the rocking chair near the stove. She picked up a little dress she had been finishing for the new baby. Sam sat in the other rocker with Quentin in his arms. The little fellow was already in his nightdress and, as his father sang his favorite lullaby, his eyes grew heavy, and he soon dropped off to sleep. After carrying him up to the loft to his crib, Sam returned to his chair, and picked up his Bible.

The evening passed quietly. But as their regular bedtime drew near, suddenly Hazel gasped, and then winced in pain. Sam looked at her in alarm.

13

"What is it?" he asked anxiously. "Have the pains started?"

"It was a sharp pain," she answered. "You don't suppose this baby is really going to decide to arrive tonight, do you?"

When another pain came a little later, Sam arose hastily, and began to bundle up in his heavy coat, boots, stocking cap and mittens.

"I mustn't wait any longer!" He looked at her, anxiety in his eyes. "I'll stop at Jess and Stella's on the way to town and ask Jess to bring Stella up here to be with you while I go for the doctor. Don't worry, Hazel, I'll hurry. You had plenty of time when Quentin was born."

The young mother dreaded being left alone, but she knew that Stella would come. They were best friends, and Stella had been with her the last time.

Sam bent to kiss his wife, "I hate to leave you alone, dear, but I don't see any other way. I'm sure Stella will get here soon. God will help us." And giving her another hug he hurried out the door.

When Sam went to the stable to harness the mare, he was horrified to find that she was not in the barn. He stumbled around in the barnyard, calling to her, but soon decided it was useless to look for her in the storm. He didn't have any time to waste. He would have to walk the ten miles to town and started out on a run.

"It's a good thing that it is all downhill," he thought, as he went loping down the road, swinging the lantern and bending his face into the storm. *If I can just get to Jess' place and ask him to take Stella back to Hazel!*

Part way down the hill, he saw the house, but it was dark. *It's late. They've already gone to bed.*

Pounding on the door, he soon heard footsteps inside. His brother opened cautiously, and then

14

exclaimed, "What on earth brings you here at this hour and in this weather?" Swinging the door open, he continued, "Come on in and warm yourself."

"I can't come in," Sam was gasping for breath. "It's Hazel! The baby is coming! I've got to get the doctor. I couldn't find Molly so I had to walk. Could you take Stella up to be with Hazel in case I don't get back in time?"

"Of course, but do you think you can make it walking to town in this storm? Maybe I should take you."

"No, you have only one horse. It's more important that someone be with Hazel. I'll make it." And Sam was off down the road, soon disappearing in the darkness.

Jess and Stella dressed hurriedly, and while he harnessed the horse and hooked it to the sleigh, she gathered a few things together. They were soon on their way up the hill to the Logan cabin. They found Hazel badly in need of help. Stella quickly took off her coat, stoked the fire, and filled up the available kettles with water to be heating. She then made Hazel as comfortable as possible. "Don't worry, Hazel. Even if the doctor doesn't make it in time, I've helped a lot of babies into this world."

Meanwhile Sam was half-walking, half-running down the road toward town in the storm. His lungs ached and his breath came in gasps, but he hurried on. *I just hope that Dr. Truax is home.* Lifting his heart to God he began to pray, "Lord, if I've ever needed you, it is now. Please help us! Help me to find the doctor and get him back up the hill in time! Please be with Hazel, and help Jess and Stella to get there quickly."

When he finally arrived at the doctor's door, he rapped loudly. There was a stirring within, and the doctor himself opened the door.

"It's my wife, Doctor! We live up on Doukhobor hill. She is in labor. My horse ran off, and I had to come on foot. Can you come with me?"

"Of course, of course," the doctor replied. "Just give me time to dress and harness up Dobbins. You won't have to walk back."

"Thank you, Lord!" Sam breathed. Dr. Truax was the well-known country doctor whom people in that valley could always count on.

It was all up hill, and with the snowstorm it seemed to Sam that they would never get there. But finally he saw the flickering light of the lamp in his own cabin. "You jump out and go on in, Doctor. I'll take care of your horse."

Stella met the doctor at the door. "Thank goodness, you made it! I think that things are going well, but I feel much better with you here."

The doctor took off his coat, and scrubbed his hands in the washbasin near the door. Stella was glad to give him her place at the bedside.

After rubbing the doctor's horse down and covering him with a blanket in the stable, Sam hurried into the house.

"How is she, Doctor?"

"Things are fine, Sam. We got here in plenty of time." Stella and the doctor worked over Hazel, and Sam paced the floor in the background. There was little he could do, except to keep the fire stoked and stay out of the way.

Time seemed to drag on forever. He was accustomed to solving the problems in his family, but this was a time he was helpless and could only pray for his wife. Finally, he drew a quick breath when he heard a different cry, a baby's cry! "Doctor! Is it over? What is it? Is the baby all right? Is Hazel all right?"

"Just a minute there, young man. One thing at a time! Yes, everyone is fine, and you have a bouncing, baby daughter!"

"Thank you, Lord," Sam breathed.

After making sure that the mother and baby were both taken care of, the doctor gave Stella last minute instructions. Then he packed up his bag and donned his heavy coat, hat and gloves to leave.

"I'll help you hitch up, Doctor. Thank you so much for coming out on a night like this."

"That's what doctors are for, Sam," the older man answered with a smile.

The doctor and his sleigh soon disappeared down the road, and Sam went back into the cabin. Stella was washing the baby and dressing her.

"She is really a little chubby, isn't she?" Stella smiled, holding the baby up for her father to see.

"She looks perfect to me," the proud father beamed. Placing the little bundle beside her mother, Stella asked, "What are you going to call her?"

"Sam has a name picked out," Hazel murmured sleepily.

"You know, long before I even knew Hazel, I had some friends with a little girl with a special name. I decided that if I ever had a daughter, she would be a special girl and I would like her to have that name. It is Alcyon. Since Hazel has a sister named Ruth we decided to call our first daughter, Alcyon Ruth. You remember that we lost our first baby daughter so we called her Evangeline, and saved this name."

"Yes, I remember that sad day," Stella replied, noticing the tears in Hazel's eyes. She remembered that Jess and Sam had built a little casket, and she lined it and dressed the baby. Hazel had fallen the day before, and the perfectly formed baby was born dead. Close family members were there to bury little Evangeline out under a tree in the yard. "But this baby is strong and healthy, this little Alcyon. Quite a name for such a little mite!"

The next morning Sam came to Hazel's bed. "How's our mommy doing?" he asked, planting a kiss on her cheek. "And how is our new little daughter?"

"We're both fine now," his wife answered, smiling. "That was pretty scary last night. When you left, I was afraid no one would get here in time, but I prayed, and it all turned out. Stella, here, was just wonderful. When she got here I wasn't afraid any more. But how did you do driving down in the storm? It seemed like a long time before you and the doctor got back."

"Didn't Stella tell you? Molly had gotten loose and I couldn't find her. I had to walk and run to town. That's one baby's birth I'll never forget! I can tell you that I did some praying, too. You know, Hazel, I've been thinking about it last night and this morning. For some reason I have the feeling that this little daughter will have some special place in God's plan. At one time while I was studying to be a nurse at Battle Creek, I wanted to be a missionary. Maybe Alcyon will fulfill that dream."

"She certainly made a big impression with her entry into the world," Hazel replied. "I just hope we can raise her, and Quentin too, to be whatever God wants them to be."

Her husband put his hand over hers. "Let's ask God to give us the help and wisdom we will need, and dedicate this new little life to Him."

Chapter 4

Doukhobor Hill

The year that Alcyon was born, 1921, the winter came early and was severe. The snow was deep and stayed well into the spring. The long winter finally passed and spring came. The baby grew fat and healthy. She spent a lot of time in her wicker baby buggy. Hazel would take her outside in it while she hung out the clothes or worked in the garden. Quentin loved to push the buggy, and his mother had to watch him closely. One day she looked up, just in time, to see him pushing the buggy, with the baby inside, toward the incline where the road started down the hill. She ran to the rescue! "No, no, Quentin! You mustn't do that! You could hurt little sister!"

"Tister want to go for ride!" he insisted!

I'll have to watch him closer, his mother realized.

The summer was a busy time. Sam spent long hours out in their woods, cutting down trees, sawing them into lengths that would fit in their stove and then chopping them into firewood. He had a neat pile along the side of the cabin and more in the lean-to by the barn. They wouldn't be cold during the coming winter.

They had a big garden that furnished their vegetables, and Hazel filled and preserved every jar for winter. Brindle's milk kept them in butter, cream and cheese. Their flock of chickens furnished their eggs. No, they wouldn't be hungry or cold!

Still, there was a nagging worry. One day Sam told his wife, "I heard today that the mill may never materialize." They had purchased this property, understanding that a sawmill was to be started nearby. Their abundance of trees could be cut and sold to the mill. What would happen to their grand plan? Their cash was getting low.

One day Hazel tucked the baby into her buggy, and with Quentin toddling along by her side, she walked down the road to visit their nearest Doukhobor neighbors. One of the younger women had been friendly to Hazel. Sometimes Freida brought her a basket of peaches or a tin of berries. In turn, Hazel helped Freida with a dress she was making.

"You sew very nice," Freida told her.

"Well, you see, I have a degree in tailoring and dress-making," Hazel explained. "Before I was married I worked in a shop."

"I have other friends who need sewing done. Would you take in some sewing?" Freida inquired.

"I don't know why not," Hazel answered.

Later, when Sam came in for supper, she told him about her visit. "You know, maybe I can make a little money sewing. I might even get some customers downtown. It's a good thing I kept my Singer sewing machine. I bought it new in Lincoln, Nebraska before Mama and Papa moved us all up to Alberta."

"I hate for you to have to do this, Hazel, but, it is true, we do need to find a way to earn some cash while waiting to see if the mill will materialize. Give it a try if you want to. During the winter I can probably help you with some of the housework. After all, you know I was a bachelor for quite a few years before I met you." He gave her a knowing smile.

It wasn't long before one of Frieda's friends brought some gingham material to Hazel. "Frieda tells me that you are an expert seamstress. I should have learned how to sew, but I don't do a very good job. Do you have time to make me a dress?"

"Sure, I can find time if you aren't in too much of a hurry. Let's see what you have." And the two young women put the material out on the table. The girl explained how she wanted the dress. Hazel knew that the Doukhobors dressed pretty much alike, and their clothes were simple and modest. It was the beginning of a little business that helped the family with cash for clothes and other incidentals. It also helped Hazel and Sam to make friends among their neighbors.

Sam and Hazel struggled through another winter. Practicing frugality, they managed to get by. Sam trapped small animals and sold the furs. But the little place on the hill was not bringing the income they had hoped for.

One day, while shopping in town, they noticed an empty building right on the main street. "You know, Sam, maybe we should inquire about that empty place. It would make a good dressmaking shop."

Sam loved the place on the hill and the log cabin they had made with their own hands. He realized that things had not turned out as well as they had hoped, but he was loath to give up. "I guess it wouldn't hurt to inquire," he conceded.

They found the owner, and he let them in to look. Hazel was hurrying through the different rooms. "Look here, Sam! There is enough room here in the back for you to set up your treatment rooms. You could practice your profession here, and I could have a dressmaking and hat shop out in front."

"It might be worth thinking about," Sam said thoughtfully. "There is even an apartment upstairs." They climbed up the stairs and saw that the three rooms would be adequate for them.

Later, riding up the hill behind Molly, the children were both sound asleep, Alcyon in her basket and Quentin with his head on his mother's lap. The couple continued talking of the possibilities of moving to town.

As the summer drew to a close, they discussed it more seriously. The shop on Main Street was still vacant, and the owner had come down on his rental price.

"Let's move to town for the winter and give it a try. We will still keep our place up here," Sam suggested one day.

"I think it is a good idea," she agreed.

His wife was happy. It would be fun for her to have her own shop. Grand Forks was a small town, and there might not be a lot of business, but it was worth a try.

Chapter 5

Leaving The Cabin

"If we are going to move we had better do it before the snow falls," Sam told Hazel after they finished putting the children to bed and were sitting in their chairs before the fire. "Even though it has been a struggle here because of the mill project failing, I'll really miss this place. I had always dreamed of building my own log cabin."

"Me, too," Hazel agreed. "It has been the first home of our own, humble as it is. We've been comfortable here, and it has been such a good place for Quentin. He has all the room he needs to play. Now that Alcyon is walking, she enjoys the outdoors too. But I really have to keep an eye on her. Yesterday, I caught her heading for the road."

"That's the worst thing about living in town." Sam was thoughtful. "The children won't have much room to play. Maybe by spring we'll decide to come back up here."

"You said that Jess could help us move next week. Can we be ready by then?" Hazel asked.

"If you can get everything packed up in the house I'll ask Jess which day he can come. Probably Monday would be best."

The next morning, after the dishes were washed, Hazel began packing up the canned fruit in the cellar. "Quentin, you watch your little sister while I go to the cellar. She is happy out in the yard playing with her toys right now."

Quentin knew that Alcyon loved to leaf through the Montgomery Ward catalogue. It would keep her occupied. He brought the big book and settled her on the step. He wanted to do some investigating on his own.

It seemed just a short time, when the four year old ran back to check on his sister. But she wasn't there. "Sister, where are you?" he called frantically. But she was nowhere to be found. He ran down to the cellar where his mother was packing fruit in boxes. "Mama! I can't find Alcyon!"

Hazel ran up to the yard where the children had been playing. She called and called, running to the barn, back into the house. "Quentin! Did you stay with her like I asked you to?"

Quentin's eyes showed his fright, "I was here part of the time. I just left for a little bit."

"Maybe she tried to go up to the woods where Papa is working," Hazel reasoned. "You had better run up there and find out."

Quentin ran toward the woods. Hazel began searching in the trees behind the house, calling over and over again. Soon she saw Sam running toward the house with Quentin. But there was no little girl with them.

"Oh Lord!" she prayed audibly. "Please help us find our baby. Please protect her."

The three searched every direction and every possible place they could think of. Hazel ran down the driveway to the main road, but she couldn't see anything in either direction.

"I'll go down to the neighbors," Sam suggested. "I don't see how she could get that far, but we have to do something." And he started down the road.

But at the first turn, he saw a most welcome sight. One of the Doukhobor men was walking up the road with a little girl by the hand. "Papa!" she cried, running to his arms. Her clothes were dirty and her face was smeared with dust.

"Where did you find her?" Sam asked the man.

"I saw this little girl walking down the road. When I got close I told my wife, 'That looks like the Logan's little girl.' She acted like she knew where she was going."

"Where were you going, Alcyon?" her father asked. "I's goin' to gamma's," she answered, with a matter-of-fact expression.

Sam thanked his neighbor and headed back up toward the cabin with Alcyon in his arms. When he came in sight of their road, Hazel and Quentin were waiting.

When Hazel saw that her husband had a child in his arms she knew that it was their lost little girl. She ran to them and took Alcyon from her father. "My baby!" she cried, the tears flowing. "Where was she?" she asked.

"She said she was going to grandma's!" Sam grinned. "I don't think she ever knew she was lost."

"But she is only two years old!" her mother exclaimed. "How would she get that idea into her head?"

"I don't know, but I think we have a daughter who has ideas of her own!"

They all walked back to the cabin. Hazel needed to finish her work in the cellar, but she decided that Alcyon would stay with her.

The rest of that week was spent preparing to leave the cabin, and moving to their apartment in town. Sam dreaded leaving the land and the little cabin where he had pinned such high hopes.

Hazel was not a stranger to moving. Her father, Fred Johnson, was an Adventist minister, and her childhood had included many moves where Father Johnson was sent to preach. It was sad to leave the cozy little cabin, but her head was full of plans, ideas of setting up her dressmaking shop and fixing up the apartment. At least there would be inside plumbing and electricity.

The morning of the move, Jess was there early to help Sam load the wagon. Jess would take the animals to his place with the farm equipment. When it was all loaded, the two men drove off toward town.

A last look around gave Hazel a pang of regret to see the little cabin left there alone and empty. She closed the door and locked it, and then called, "Come on, children. We are ready."

Quentin crawled up into the buggy, and Hazel lifted the little girl, placing her in the middle. Taking the reins from the hitching post, she seated herself and said. "Gettyup, Molly", and they were soon trotting down the hill.

The clippity clop of the horse's hooves on the gravel road almost sang a tune, as Hazel thought about this new adventure. They were on their way to a new chapter in their lives.

Chapter 6

Sam to the Rescue

By the time the buggy pulled up in front of the store building in town, the men were already unloading the wagon. "We need you to tell us where to put things, Hazel."

She jumped down from the buggy, tied Molly to a hitching post, and lifted the children down. "I'm coming."

"Quentin, you and Alcyon can play in the back room here downstairs," she told him as she led them to the area that Sam would use for his treatment rooms.

The two men were struggling with the heavy cook stove on the stairway. As soon as they began to bring up the boxes, Hazel was ready to start unpacking them. Since that one room would serve for both kitchen and living, she was eager to make it look like home, even to a white cloth on the table.

By supper time the little Logan family was installed in their new home, the fire crackling in the wood range, and vegetable soup simmering on the back of the stove. Hazel had baked bread before moving, so their meal was complete.

With breakfast over the next morning, Hazel and Sam put their energies to setting up the shop and treatment rooms.

"Quentin, why don't you take your sister up on the stair landing and play with your Tiddly Winks?" Hazel told her son. The stairs were covered with a worn, red carpet runner. The landing, where the stairs turned, was spacious, and warmed with the sun shining through a large window. In the days following, the children often gravitated to that special place on the landing with their toys.

Sitting around their supper table one evening, Sam's brow was furrowed. "Our funds are dangerously low, Hazel. I hope that business begins to pick up soon." His expression showed concern.

"I will be finishing several garments this week, and that will bring in a few dollars," Hazel added. "We still have lots of canned food and the potatoes, squash, carrots and turnips from last summer's garden, so we won't go hungry, but that won't pay the rent."

"I'll bring enough wood down from the mountain to last us through the winter," Sam promised. "I'm not sure this was a good idea to come to British Columbia, especially to this area. Of course, we haven't given ourselves enough time to really know how things will turn out."

"It is a little discouraging," Hazel answered thoughtfully. "I've been getting some sewing to do for people, but not enough to really keep me busy. You know, some of the ladies stop in here, and just like to sit around visiting. I keep hearing the comment, 'Grand Forks is dead!' I'm sure many people are struggling like we are."

"Well, we haven't been here long enough to know how things will go, or even to be sure the mill is not going to materialize. Let's just do our best and leave things in God's hands." Sam had thought and prayed about their situation. *God must have an answer.*

Sam rose from his chair and headed downstairs to bring up more wood for the stove. While he was gone,

Hazel heard the bell ring at the front door. Soon Sam was running up the stairs. "That was Joe Williams. Their little boy, Tommy, is sick. They want me to come. I think it is the influenza. There is a lot of it going around."

"Let me help you get your things together. You'll need the fomentation cloths and you'd better take the steamer. They might not have a large enough kettle." Hazel talked as she bustled about.

As Sam walked through his front gate, Joe Williams came out to meet him. "Thanks for coming so quick, Mr. Logan. Do you think you can help Tommy? He is delirious with fever."

"What did the doctor tell you, Joe?"

"He said it is influenza, but that it has gone into pneumonia. Said it seems to have to run its course. He gave us some powder to give him, but it hasn't helped." Mary Williams sat on the edge of the bed, bathing the little fellow's face with cold rags. Her face was drawn and worried.

"Get your fire going, Joe. I'll need some hot water." Soon he had his steamer with the fomentations heating on the black cook stove, and the steam was rising.

When the wool cloths were hot, Sam carefully wrapped the first one in a dry towel and placed it all the way down the little boy's back. He kept his hand running under it to be sure it didn't burn. Three times he changed to another hot one. Placing his hand on the child's forehead, he noted, "He's beginning to perspire. This will break the fever." Then he ran a cold cloth quickly over the now rosy back and dried it briskly with another dry towel. "Now, turn him over," he instructed the mother. "We will do the same thing to his chest."

Sam stayed with the Williams family through the night, repeating the treatment every two hours.

As dawn began to break, he folded up the equipment and prepared to leave. He had sent Mary to get some rest. Tommy was sleeping peacefully now, and the fever was down. "I'll come over later in the day, Joe, to give him another treatment. But I am sure he is out of danger. Don't let him get up or get chilled. Give him lots of water and juices to drink."

"I don't know how to thank you, Mr. Logan. We were afraid Tommy was going to die," Joe said earnestly, shaking Sam's hand. "We don't have much money, but we'll find some way to pay you!"

"The important thing now is to get Tommy well," Sam assured him as he opened the door to leave.

Hazel was cooking breakfast as her husband wearily climbed the stairs to the apartment. "What happened? How is he?"

"Tommy is going to make it if he doesn't get a relapse," he answered as he sank into a chair. "He was a very sick little boy. It is really amazing how these Battle Creek treatments bring such quick results. People don't understand their value yet, but I've never seen them to fail. They bring the body's own resources into play."

"After you eat, why don't you crawl into bed, Sam? I can call you if any one needs you." He didn't need urging. Later in the day, he went back to the Williams. Tommy was begging to get up.

"I can't believe it!" his mother exclaimed. "I can hardly keep him in bed."

"These treatments are very effective in treating influenza and pneumonia," Sam told her, "but you need to know that it is God's blessing that really makes the difference. I always ask God to help me."

There were other cases of influenza in the little town. The word spread, and Sam was going from one sick bed to another with his fomentation cloths and steamer. None of those who received the treatments died. Even the good doctor was calling on Sam for some of his patients.

Chapter 7

"Grand Forks is Dead"

"When will it be Sabbath?" Quentin asked one Friday. The children were playing with their blocks on the floor in the shop where their mother was working.

Alcyon, who was talking more and more, lifted her eyes from her doll she was undressing. "When be Sabbat'?"

Their mother was sitting nearby, basting the hem of a dress. "It will be tomorrow. Do you children like Sabbath?"

"Oh, yes," Quentin replied. "I like our class. Mrs. Ellis tells us such good stories."

That evening, the little family gathered in their warm sitting area upstairs to have their sundown worship and welcome in the Sabbath hours. Sam and Hazel sang several of the children's songs they had learned, and Quentin, who could already carry a tune, joined in. Little Alcyon sang lustily, knowing some of the words, but badly off tune. When their mother tucked them into bed that night they were anxious for the morning, so they could go to Sabbath School.

"Sabbat' School today?" Alcyon toddled into her parents' bedroom early the next morning.

Sam was already out in the kitchen making a fire when Hazel opened her eyes to see her little daughter standing there in her nightgown. "Yes, you little rascal! We are going to Sabbath School, but it is still cold. Papa is making the fire. Let's wait until the fire makes the room warm. Here, come into bed with Mama."

Alcyon was wide-awake and wanted everyone to get ready to go to Sabbath School. Sam soon had the stove crackling and Hazel knew he would have the oatmeal cooking. After all, he prided himself on being a good cook. He had been a bachelor long enough to learn.

Finally, the little family was all dressed in their Sabbath best and on their way. The Ellises lived in town just a short walk away. Several families had already arrived. There were Mr. and Mrs. Foster, Sam's parents, and the Cooper family, as well as others the Logans didn't know as well.

The children were taken into the dining room where Mrs. Ellis had a low table made into a sand box. After singing several children's songs, she sat the children around the table and began telling the Bible story of the week. Alcyon and Quentin were fascinated as their teacher placed the cutouts she had prepared to illustrate the story of Baby Moses. It left a picture in Alcyon's mind that she never forgot.

The Logan family became part of the village life, and the children felt at home, playing indoors in bad weather and playing on the sidewalk in front on good days. Alcyon loved to sit on one of the worktables with her doll, pretending to make clothes for her with scraps of material that her mother gave her. She chattered away to the customers, never seeming to know a stranger.

One winter day, the family was gathered in the kitchen while Hazel prepared the meal. The fire was going good, but the room was still cool. Sam opened the oven door to heat the room faster. Alcyon was in her high chair with her back towards the stove. Sam had gone into the bedroom and Hazel was busy with her cooking, when she heard a crash and then a scream.

She exclaimed, "What happened?" She turned to see the high chair on its back, with Alcyon on the floor screaming and crying, blood streaming from the back of her head. Quentin had stood on the spindle on the back of the high chair and it had gone over on top of him. The little boy was picking himself up, but Alcyon lay there crying. She had fallen, hitting her head on the corner of the oven door.

Sam came running, and they began putting cold clothes on her head. It was a big gash, but the blood finally stopped and Hazel held the little girl until she stopped crying. Quentin was crying, too. "I didn't mean to hurt her."

"I know you didn't, Sonny," his mother comforted. "But you will learn never to stand on the high chair again, won't you?"

He nodded tearfully.

One day Sam came into the shop. He had been to his parents' house. "Pa and Ma are going to move to Oregon," he announced. "Remember they told us recently that my sister Laura and her family have moved to a little town west of Salem called Falls City? They bought a big ranch on the hill above the village and are going to have a fruit farm. They are urging the folks to move down there."

"Well, that's news," Hazel replied. "I know Ma mentioned the other day that Pa's eyes are getting so bad, he really can't keep up their place any more."

"It seems that there is a nice little house on an acre of land, just up the hill from the main street in Falls City."

"When do they plan to go?" Hazel queried.

"I guess as soon as they can sell their place here and make arrangements."

When the last customer had gone, they continued their conversation about Ma and Pa Logan's move back to the States. Sam had been raised in Kansas, and the family had all migrated to Canada several years before.

Hazel had secretly harbored the hope that someday they might move back to the land of her birth. They had been in Grand Forks for a year now. The lumber mill was obviously not going to materialize, and their experiment in town had provided only enough to barely make ends meet.

Hazel reminded her husband, "I guess that what people say is true, Grand Forks is dead!"

"Ma and Pa wondered if we plan to stay on here, or if we might consider going to Oregon."

"What did you tell them?"

"Well, of course I told them that we have been concerned about our finances and our future here, but we hadn't seriously considered leaving. What do you think?"

Hazel pondered that question. "Well, I guess I would have to say that we need to do something. I've been hoping that business would get better. Going to Oregon sounds appealing."

Sam sat in one of the rockers in deep thought. "Let's think about it some more. We would have to do some inquiring about opportunities."

Later at the supper table, Sam asked Quentin, "Would you like to ask the blessing tonight?"

They all bowed their heads and Quentin began in a serious tone, "Grand Forks is dead, Amen."

It was hard to keep their smiles hidden, but they realized that even their little son had been listening and caught the mood of the village. It was the beginning of the change that would make a big impact on their lives.

Chapter 8

Off To Oregon

Sam and Hazel talked of little else for the next few weeks. Actually, Hazel was more interested in the move than Sam. One day she suggested, "Why don't you take a trip to Salem. See if God seems to open the doors. We want to do the right thing."

Sam made the trip to look the situation over. When he came home he was enthusiastic. "You will like Oregon, especially Salem in the Willamette valley."

"Did you find a way to get started there?" she asked anxiously.

"That's the good part! I found a place in Salem, just 28 miles from Falls City where Ma and Pa are. An older doctor wants to retire and is willing to rent us his office complex. There is also an apartment with plenty of room for us to live in."

Sam and Hazel talked until late that night. The decision was made. They would move to Oregon!

They were able to rent their cabin on the hill to friends. The next few weeks were busy ones, selling most of their furniture and shipping the rest. Tickets were purchased for their train trip south.

Finally, the last bag was packed and friends saw them off. The Logans found their way into a coach on the train where the seats were upholstered in red velvet. Sam decided on a double seat, one facing the other. A small straw suitcase contained their lunch food, and it was placed on the overhead shelf. The children sat with their faces glued to the window as the train began to gain speed.

Before long Hazel suggested, "It's warm in here, Sam. Could you open the window?"

As Sam opened the heavy window Quentin stuck his head out, but he drew it back in a hurry crying, "Ouch! My eyes!"

"That's the cinders from the coal burning engine," Sam exclaimed, slamming the window down. "We'll have to leave the window shut."

Three-year-old Alcyon fastened her eyes on a woman in the seat in front of theirs. She looked to her father and said in a loud voice, "Papa, look! There's a lady with a man's head on!"

Her mother hushed her up but not before the woman turned around with a cold stare. Short bobs were just coming into style, but Hazel wore long hair, and Alcyon had never seen a woman with short hair.

Alcyon could nap on the seat facing her parents, but Quentin didn't want to miss anything. The train stopped at small stations to pick up passengers. Then the whistle would blow and the cars jerk as they began to pick up speed again.

"I'm hungry," Alcyon informed her mother.

"Me, too," Quentin said. Hazel pulled down the lunch case and passed out the boiled eggs, sandwiches and apples.

As night came on, the conductor lit the kerosene lantern hanging from the ceiling of the coach. Alcyon slept on the seat in front of her parents and Quentin found space on a nearby seat. Their first train ride was an adventure for the children, but Hazel was happy when they finally came into the station in Salem.

She was delighted with Oregon. Their hopes were high. Sam could now practice the profession he was trained for. He would have a facility where physical therapy and Battle Creek treatments were given. Hazel could keep house and care for her children, and she could still do dressmaking on the side.

Chapter 9

The Truck Episode

Back in Central Oregon the Fleck family sat around the supper table. Kenneth had just filled his plate. "Mama, when is March 13?"

She smiled and asked him, "Now, why would you ask that? Would it have something to do with your birthday?"

The boy grinned and admitted, "Well, I was just wondering about something. Can I tell you what I want to do on my birthday?"

His father held his fork in mid-air and turned to his son. "March 13 is next Monday. You can always tell us what you would like to do. It won't hurt anything to do that. Tell us what you have been thinking."

Young Kenneth thought a minute, trying to decide how to say it. "I was just wondering if I could go and visit school with Melvin. I'll be 7 and old enough now to start next school year."

Besides James, Ida, Kenneth and his 3-year-old little sister, Jean, James' nephew, Melvin, 13, was there. His mother, Emma, was James' older sister. She and her husband, Scotty, had homesteaded 2 miles down the road from the Flecks. When Emma sickened, she went to Portland for treatment. Scotty found it difficult to care for their one son and still go back and forth to Portland. When Ida suggested, "Let Melvin come and stay with us," Scotty was relieved. By then Scotty had found work near his wife in Portland and made other arrangements for his farm. Emma's sickness led to an early death, leaving her son motherless. Melvin stayed on with his uncle and family, until he finished his eight grades in the country school.

"So you want to go and visit school?" His father smiled with a twinkle in his eye. "Well now, that is an interesting request. What do you think, Mama?"

Kenneth knew that was a good sign. His mother usually tried to agree with him. "Maybe it would be a good idea. Then he wouldn't feel so strange next fall. But first, we need to send a note and ask the teacher."

By Monday morning it was all arranged. Melvin was happy for his company. Ida fixed two lunches that morning instead of one. In the meantime she was giving her active son some needed counsel about how to conduct himself at school.

While they were still at the breakfast table, James had an idea that he knew the boys would be happy about. "Melvin, why don't you boys ride Maude to school today? She is reliable, and there is a place to stable her while you are in school?"

"Thanks, Uncle James. We would like that. Kenneth can hang on behind me."

Both Ida and James stood in the yard watching the two boys ride off down the dirt road. Melvin usually walked the two and a quarter miles to school.

It was a brisk, but sunny spring day. About half way to school a large coyote appeared on the other side of the ditch that ran parallel to the road. Melvin quickened their pace and soon they were galloping at full speed, racing the coyote for nearly a quarter of a mile.

Nearing the school Kenneth's heart beat in anticipation. It had seemed he would never get old enough to go to school. At least he would have one day to know what it was like.

The teacher of this one room country school met Kenneth at the door while his cousin went to tie up the horse.

"I'm Miss Wilkens," she said. "You must be Kenneth Fleck. Welcome to our school today. You can sit right over here in this seat by the window."

Kenneth was in his glory. He was a big boy now, and he would show the teacher and his parents that he was big enough to go to school. Miss Wilkens brought him a first grade reader. "Here, Kenneth, maybe you can follow along as the first grade have their reading class. Someone will help you."

His mother had read to him for years and helped him to know some words. He found it easy to follow as the other students read the simple words. He watched and listened carefully as they reviewed the alphabet. Then when the first grade arithmetic was put on the board, he copied it carefully on the tablet his mother had sent with him. He even raised his hand to answer some questions.

Before the day was over, Miss Wilkens wrote a note to his parents. "I don't see any reason why your boy can't continue coming to school the rest of this year. He fits in real well and learns fast."

When Ida handed the note to James that evening, he beamed with pride. "Don't tell anyone, Ida, but remember I always told you that boy is smart! But not because he's ours!"

Kenneth was thrilled to know he could go back to school the next morning, and the next and the next until the end of the school year. He and Melvin didn't ride the horse every day, but the trip through the countryside seemed a short distance to the boys as they skipped along, running part of the way.

At the end of the year, when the parents came for the final program, Miss Wilkens came to them. "I think you should take some books home, and let Kenneth read them this summer. I'll send the second grade books, too."

It was a busy summer for the boy. His father needed his help on the farm, and he wanted to spend all the time he could with his books.

He was sitting in the living area one afternoon, when his mother called to him. "Someone just drove up. Go see who it is."

He could hardly believe his eyes. There at their gate was a Model T Ford with his father at the wheel! "Papa, Papa! Where did you get the car?"

His mother was expecting James home with the car, but she wanted Kenneth to be surprised. It wasn't a new car, didn't even have a top to it, but it was as good as new to the boy. He ran and jumped in the front seat beside his father. "Take me for a ride!"

"Well, I haven't been driving this thing very long, but I think I have the hang of it. We'll go up to the top of the hill to where we can turn around."

Kenneth could hardly sleep that night thinking about their new car. "I wish Melvin was here to see it," he said to himself. Melvin had gone to Columbia Academy. He was going to work and go to school that next term.

Every opportunity he could find, Kenneth rode along with his father that summer, always taking note of everything that James did. He asked questions, wanting to know everything about running that new automobile.

During the summer James hired a young man to help with the harvest and other work around the farm. Jeff had an old truck that he kept parked in the yard. Kenneth liked to go with Jeff whenever the truck was employed for various errands in the area. With Jeff, too, Kenneth was full of questions. He watched how the truck was started, where the brake was and the gas peddle. He even learned about the gears.

When school started that fall, Kenneth went into the third grade. Miss Wilkens found him to be a quick learner, but also a boy full of ideas.

He had just poked the boy in front of him with his pencil, when Miss Wilkens sharp eyes fastened on him, "Kenneth, will you please go and stand in that corner with your face to the wall until I tell you to leave?" He was learning what the corners of the room were used for.

One day, walking home from school, he came by the Opsund home just down the hill from the Flecks. He saw his mother out in their garden talking to Mrs. Opsund. She waved to him, and he went on home. Since he found the house empty, he walked around the yard, looking for something to do.

There sat Jeff's truck, with the key in it. Kenneth climbed in, barely able to look up and out the front window. He remembered all the steps that Jeff had to do to start the truck, and he began experimenting. He was surprised how easy it was to get it started.

Down at the Opsund's, Ida heard the truck start, and, horror of horrors, it started down the hill. "Oh my! Kenneth has gotten into that truck!" As she watched, her heart nearly stopped. There was nothing she could do but stand and watch with her heart in her mouth. "He'll kill himself!" she shouted.

But soon she saw the truck turn around and start back up the hill. By then she was running home. She could barely see a little head at the driver's seat. By the time she got there, the truck had been backed into its regular spot, and Kenneth was dismounting. When he saw his mother coming up the hill, out of breath, he knew he was in big trouble, but it had been so much fun to drive that truck!

"Kenneth! What in the world are you doing? You could have been killed!"

"No, Mama. I've watched Jeff lots of times. I know how to drive the truck!"

When his father heard the story that evening, he was nonplused to know what to do. Secretly, he was amused that this little fellow, just seven years old, could pull off a trick like that. But there had to be some consequences. "It's going to take some doing to raise that boy to manhood," he told Ida that evening in their bedroom.

Winter came early that next fall. By Thanksgiving time there was snow on the ground. James and Ida were struggling to make it on the farm. There was no extra money for unnecessary things, sometimes not even enough for the necessities.

Kenneth had grown out of his boots, and Ida knew he couldn't walk through the snow without them. She called, "Kenneth, come here and sit down on the chair. I need to wrap your feet. The snow is deep this morning." She had brought some burlap from the barn and began wrapping the burlap around his shoes, up over his pants to his knees. "That will help to keep your feet dry. We'll have to make this do until we can afford some boots for you."

Kenneth got up to walk on his "new boots" laughing. "There were some other kids with these kinds of boots yesterday at school." Apparently, he felt right in style.

During that winter on the prairie, the wind would sometimes howl around the house. Sleeping up in his cozy bed under the eaves, it seemed to Kenneth that the house would blow over with the wind. He was sure he felt the house shake. "Papa!" he would call. "Will the wind blow the house down?" The howling wind in the night was a terror to him that he remembered all his life.

"No, Son. This house is solid. I built it with my own hands."

Kenneth and his father kept busy, bringing in the wood and keeping the fires stoked in the kitchen range and the heater in the parlor. Even in the snowstorms, and when the wild winds blew over the prairies, their home on Lone Juniper Farm was a haven for Kenneth and his family.

Chapter 10

The Model T Goes to Church

Ida and James were the only members of their church in that area. They wanted their children to know what it meant to keep the Sabbath and worship God on that day. Early on they developed the custom of gathering the family together in the parlor on Sabbath mornings.

James might announce, "Kenneth, you can be the superintendent this morning."

The boy would stand up as if he were in a church and announce the opening hymn. His mother played the piano, and they would stand and sing one of the familiar hymns out of the hymnal.

Kenneth would announce, "Jean will recite the memory verse for this week." Jean would stand and recite the verse.

Then Kenneth might say, "Ida Fleck will tell the Bible story for today."

The Little Friend, that came through the mail, was used for their Sabbath School. Kenneth knew all the memory verses, and Jean learned them as soon as she was old enough. The parents did all they could to provide the atmosphere of a real Sabbath School.

When spring came again Ida asked her husband, "Do you think we could take the Model T to Bend to church? It would be so wonderful to visit a real Sabbath School and church."

"Yes, I think our Lizzy would make it. We would need to start early." The first time they ventured that far in their old Model T, it was exciting for the whole family. Kenneth and Jean rode in the open back seat, but as happy as if they were in a limousine.

The church people were delighted to have them come. Sometimes the Flecks gave the special music, a duet by Ida and James, and sometimes the children sang one of their songs. Early on, the parents knew that Kenneth had a special talent for singing. His voice was sweet and clear.

He learned to chord on the piano, and pick out his chords until he became quite proficient. But Ida thought he should learn to read music. She taught him to play some simple tunes, reading the notes.

They went to Redmond or Bend more often. They began to go occasionally to shop in the bigger stores. Ida found a piano teacher for Kenneth in Madras, and for one season he had lessons once a week. But he still preferred to chord and pick out tunes by ear while his father played his violin. Father and son spent many happy hours during the long winter evenings playing together in this way.

At the supper table one evening Kenneth had a bright idea. "I've been wondering if I could stay up all night sometime. Could I please do that tonight?"

James looked at his son. "Why would you want to do that?"

"I just want to see if I can do it."

"What do you think, Ida?" James really thought she wouldn't approve.

"I suppose it won't hurt anything to let him try it."

Bedtime came and the parents went up to their room. Kenneth started out playing on the piano. Then he read awhile. He practiced reciting poems he was learning in school. His parents listened to the noise going on downstairs. "I wonder how long this will go on," James laughed. "That boy has more ideas than a barrel of monkeys."

The noise continued downstairs, but after midnight things began to quiet down. Finally, about 2:00 A.M. there was silence below. James crept down the stairs. There was his son, sitting in a chair, sound asleep. He carried him up to his bed still asleep. In the morning Kenneth wondered how he got there.

"Do you want to stay up again tonight?" his father asked him.

Somewhat abashed, Kenneth shook his head, no.

The spring he was ten, Kenneth finished the fifth grade. That summer he was old enough to be his father's right hand. He drove the teams out in the field, and he drove the Model T around the farm, doing errands for his father.

One day, just after dinner, James looked out the window. "What is that boy doing!" Ida came running, but by then James was out the door. Kenneth had found a big barrel and thought it would be fun to get in and roll down the hill. He was already in; just his head sticking out, and the barrel had started rolling, when James sprinted to catch him before it got to rolling fast.

"What in the world were you thinking?" he asked the boy. "You could have killed yourself. Didn't you realize there are big fence posts and rocks at the bottom of the hill?"

Back in the house, James told Ida, "That was a close one. God must have made me see him in time. He could have been killed!"

Ken loved to take his 22 single shot rifle and Buster, and roam the hills. He knew every hill and valley for miles around. Those were times he began to think about serious things, to recite in his mind the scripture he had memorized and poems he had learned in school.

One day, sitting on a rock he got an idea. "I would like to make up a program. I could invite the neighbors, and maybe even some of our friends from Redmond or Bend might come."

For weeks he worked on his project. He planned a varied program, some religious songs and Bible stories and verses, and some secular. He had a little printing set and with that he made up his list. He was to do the entire program.

When he presented the plan to his parents, they gave their approval. "Your birthday will be soon. Why don't you have it on your birthday?" his mother suggested.

He didn't need much help, but Ida and James cooperated wherever they could. It was his twelfth birthday the night of the program. He had an audience of 15 or 20 people. Each had a printed program. He played and sang. He could play the piano by ear enough to accompany himself on the songs he knew. He told Bible stories, and recited scripture. He played some secular music too.

His poems consisted of "Bingen on the Rhine", "The Village Blacksmith", "The Puzzled Dutchman", "The Dashing Ride of Jenny McNeil", and others. Altogether the visitors felt they had enjoyed a wonderful evening. To finish it off, his mother served refreshments.

It was a milestone in his life, and more than one of the visitors made the remark, "That boy will be a preacher some day."

Chapter 11

Who Sleeps on the Other Side?

"What would you think about going to school at Columbia Academy next year?" his father asked Kenneth one morning after his eighth grade graduation.

"Could I do that?" Kenneth's eyes brightened up.

"We are considering it, Son. You could stay with Grandma Lashier."

"Oh, I'd like that."

Ida's mother, now widowed, lived near Columbia Academy, in the village of Meadow Glade, near Vancouver, Washington.

Ida was sure her mother would want Kenneth to be with her, and had written her. When the answer came back, she opened the envelope eagerly.

"Of course, I want Kenneth to come and stay with me. I have just rented out part of my house, but we can remodel the small storage room in the back yard for a kitchen. We'll manage fine."

Arrangements were made. His father decided to take him down in the old Chrysler that had replaced the Model T. "We'll all go and take Kenneth to Meadow Glade."

"I'll feel a lot better if we can help him get installed," his mother added.

His excitement ran high, thinking of all the things he could do in a school like Columbia Academy. But when his bags were packed, and he walked out of his little room under the eves, he had a lump in his throat.

Every one was in the car, but Kenneth hadn't come.

His father called, "Kenneth! Where are you?"

But he didn't answer. Going around to the back of the house James found the boy sitting on the step, holding his dog in his arms crying. "I wish I didn't have to leave Rover," he said through his tears. Old Buster had been replaced by a younger dog that Kenneth claimed as his own.

"I know it's hard to leave Rover, Son, but he'll be here when you come back."

"But what will he do without me? He goes every place with me."

James comforted him as well as he could. Finally, Kenneth dried his tears and went bravely to the car for his new adventure, his first time away from home.

Grandma was waiting with open arms. Her youngest son, Harold, was away at college. Ida's sister, Mamie, had married and now had her own family. Kenneth would be company for Grandma.

The family stayed for several days. His father helped him to register at the academy, that was also a boarding school, and Kenneth went to the first social of the year, the traditional handshake. It was a time to get acquainted. He soon made friends. Evern Budd lived nearby and they became friends right away.

This was the middle of the great depression. When Grandma rented her house to help with her finances, she was left with only one bedroom. "You can put your clothes on this side of the room," she told her grandson. "We only have one bed, but it is a full size. I'll divide it down the middle with some blankets rolled up, and we'll get along fine."

Kenneth wasn't too thrilled with the arrangement, but there wasn't anything else they could do. Grandma was willing to take him in, and he should be thankful.

Kenneth and Evern rigged up a wire stretching between their houses that they could send signals on. One day when they were connecting the wire to Grandma's house, they were in the bedroom. Evern looked around, "Is this your room?"

"Yes, it is," hoping there would be no more questions asked.

"Where do you want the wire put?"

"Put it right here on this side where I sleep."

"Well, who sleeps on the other side?"

His face red with embarrassment, Kenneth answered, "Grandma sleeps on that side." Up to that time in his life this was his most embarrassing moment for the 13-year-old boy.

Grandma fixed up the storeroom for their kitchen and eating area. By the time she got through it was comfortable and cozy. She cooked for her young grandson like she would for company. He would never forget those good meals that only Grandma could make. He was her first grand child, and he knew as long as she lived that she would do anything in the world that she could for him.

Her house was on a five-acre tract, and in the back was a grove of trees. Grandma had fixed up a special private cove there where she would go to pray. Often she would ask, "Kenneth, do you want to go and pray with me?" And he loved to go.

Grandma prayed to her Father in heaven as if He were right there with them. She prayed with her whole heart, mentioning every one of her family by name. She prayed for God's work around the world, and for His ministers. And she prayed for Kenneth that he would become a faithful worker for God. Her prayers were sometimes long, but Kenneth never failed to feel the closeness of God to them there in their bower. Then she would ask him to pray. His prayers were short, but he was learning a lot about talking to God.

Kenneth soon became a part of the school family. Even though he lived in the village, and not in the dormitory, he was included in all the activities. He especially loved to go to the Friday evening vespers. He was beginning to think of his future. People often asked him if he was going to be a minister.

Why do people ask me that? He wondered. *Is that what I have to do?*

It was in the Academy where music became an important part of his life. People soon learned that Kenneth Fleck had a beautiful tenor voice. He was asked to be part of the school male quartet along with Fred Lengel, Virgil House, and Lloyd Atkins. Soon the quartet was invited to go to other churches to sing.

Kenneth's friendly personality won him many friends. But there were moments when he felt pangs of homesickness and thought; *I wonder what the folks are doing today. I wish I could see Rover.*

As the school year drew to a close, he began to look forward to going home for the summer. When his parents came for him, he told his friends good-by, not realizing the changes coming in his life before he would see Meadow Glade and Columbia Academy again.

Chapter 12

Home in Salem

My father never tired of telling me about the night when he had to run and walk ten miles down the hill for the doctor. There were other stories, too, of my earliest days in Canada. As I grew up I enjoyed looking at the family album of myself as a baby, of the log house, even of myself as a toddler, looking through the Montgomery Ward catalogue.

My earliest memories were in the apartment in Grand forks. Certain pictures seemed to stand out. I remember sitting up on my mother's sewing table, playing with scraps of cloth, and trying to pin them onto my doll.

But one of the best memories was of sitting at the sand table in Mrs. Ellis' house in our home Sabbath School.

I learned of other bits and pieces of our early years up on Doukhobor Hill in the log cabin. Not long ago, in going through old family papers, I found my mother's diary that she kept up there on the hill.

In later years, with my mother along, we went back to Grand Forks and up Doukhobor hill. She guided us right to the old place. The buildings were still standing, although abandoned. It was there that she told me the story of when I was lost, and the Doukhobor neighbor brought me up the hill. "I remember so well," she said, "of the panic I felt and how relieved I was, standing right here seeing your father come carrying you back up the road."

I've always been thankful for that little glimpse into my first years. Somehow, walking around that place, I almost felt like I had come home.

It wasn't long after coming to Oregon that I got another bump on the head because of trying to follow my mischievous brother.

One day Quentin and some friends were playing in one of the vacant rooms in our building, where there was a bed with only a link spring. The boys started to jump on it, having great fun. I came in and climbed up on the bed. When the jumping started again, I was thrown to the cement floor on my head. I lay quiet with my head bleeding.

Quentin jumped down, running for our mother. "Mama, come quick! Alcyon is hurt!" By the time Mama arrived, I was opening my eyes and crying. All the children were sent home

"Go call Papa quick!" she told my brother.

Papa came running. He examined me and found a large bump that was bleeding on the back of my head. "I think she will be all right, but we need to keep a cold cloth on it for awhile. I hope all these bumps on her head don't have a permanent effect. Maybe they will make her extra smart!"

My mother didn't see the humor. "I just hope she survives with her rambunctious brother!"

Later that day Mama told Papa, "I don't know what we will do. Alcyon follows Quentin wherever he goes, and she is too little for some of his play."

One day Papa was busy in his office and Mama was sewing. The afternoon was getting long, and we were tired of our toys. Quentin took me by the hand out to the back hall. He pointed up to a bag on the wall. "See that bag. I saw Papa put some money in it. Let's see if we can reach it." He pulled a chair up to the wall and stood up on it, but he still could not reach the bag. Running into another room he found a stool and put it on the chair. "Here, you hold the stool while I climb up." I followed his orders, and he climbed to where he could reach the bag. Then, just barely reaching it, he put in his hand and pulled out a silver dollar. "Look, we can go and buy some candy with this!"

Leaving the chair and the stool he took me by the hand, went out the back door and around the block. There was a little candy store where a heavyset man with an apron stood behind the counter. Quentin pointed to some penny candies in a jar. The man put some of them in a sack and handed it to us. Quentin proudly handed him the dollar, took the bag, and we walked on up the block, eating the candy, never waiting for change.

The man must have grinned. "They must have slipped that dollar out of someplace they weren't supposed to!"

Later that day Mama found the chair and stool under the moneybag. She told our father when he came in from work. "Have you counted the tithe money lately? It looks to me like the children have been into it."

After checking the bag, he called his little son into the bedroom. "Did you get into the bag up on the wall today?"

Quentin hung his head and nodded. Papa went on. "Did you know that that money belongs to Jesus?" He went on to explain what tithe money was. "What did you do with the money?"

"We bought candy," Quentin confessed.

Papa dealt with Quentin to teach him a lesson. I stood anxiously outside the closed door. I thought I would be next, but Papa must have thought I was too young to take any blame. But I suffered along with him with my ear glued to the door. It was a good lesson we never forgot.

Chapter 13

Great Grandpa Stover

"Wake up, children! It's time to get up. Your breakfast is ready." We were going to a real Sabbath School.

Before moving to Oregon we had only gone to Sabbath School at the Ellis' house. This would be a new experience.

The Salem church, during my childhood, was one of the largest in the Oregon Conference. There was a whole roomful of children in the kindergarten department. There were tables and little chairs, and a leader who knew many children's songs.

Sabbath was a special day for us. Although it was at least a mile to church, our family walked. There were streetcars on some main streets, but not to the church.

Quentin and I had never heard of a camp meeting. When the date was announced at church, it was discussed at home. Of course our parents remembered camp meetings in their younger days. My mother's father was an Adventist minister in Minnesota. She remembered going early to camp meeting for tent pitch.

"We always looked forward to that," she told us. "In those days my mother worked for days, cooking, baking and sewing. We went in a wagon pulled by horses, and our cow was tied on behind. At the site, there was always a field close-by where people could pasture their cows, and go to milk them morning and night."

My father had many stories to tell about camp meetings, too. "When I studied at Battle Creek College I went to camp meeting and heard Mrs. White preach."

Our first camp meeting was in Forest Grove, Oregon. We went early Sabbath morning and arrived in time for Sabbath School. There was a huge kindergarten tent. That was an awesome experience for me.

I met cousins I didn't know before. But the most unforgettable experience was when my father told us, "Your great-grandfather is here, and he wants to meet you. He is Grandma Logan's father. His name is Grandpa Stover."

Then he explained that Grandpa Stover had been a pioneer minister. He led us up to the front of the main tent where a special chair had been placed just below the rostrum. There he sat, an old man with a long flowing beard, dressed in his preacher clothes. I was awestruck and stood looking at him.

"Come, Alcyon, Grandpa Stover wants to see you. Come closer."

His words are still fresh in my memory, as he reached out and put his hand on my head. "So this is Sam's girl. May God bless you, little dear."

Then it was Quentin's turn, and behind him some of our cousins were lined up. Most of my father's siblings had moved to Falls City and came to campmeeting.

A large portrait of Grandpa and Grandma Stover, that always hung in my Grandma Logan's parlor, hangs in our living room today. I am reminded of this ancestor who preached about Jesus' soon coming long before I was born, and who died waiting for that day. He is one person I hope to meet one day soon, and I will tell him how Ken and I followed his example.

Chapter 14

She's Too Young

When Quentin went off to school for his first grade, I felt left out. "Why can't I go, too?" I asked.

"You will go to school when you are old enough," Mama assured me. "Maybe Quentin will bring home some of his books and let you look at them."

"Don't forget to bring a book home for me to see," I reminded him as he left for school.

The Salem church was constructed with the first floor reserved for a school. The lower grades included the first six, and the second room had grades 7, 8, and 9.

When my father changed his business to a place downtown, we moved to a house, closer to the church.

I kept reminding my brother to bring his books home for me to see. Eventually he did, and I was fascinated. I loved to look through the pictures, and would beg for someone to read the stories to me. As they read I tried to follow the words.

The following year, when it was time for school to start, I saw the new clothes that Quentin was getting for school. I saw his tablets, crayons, and pencil box and was green with envy. "Why can't I go? I'm big enough."

My parents talked it over. Papa seemed to be more convinced than Mama that it might not be a bad idea. "She is tall for her age, and she will be six in November. She can already read Quentin's first reader."

In the end I won out, and happily marched off to school one morning with my father to enroll me. I stood by the teacher's desk as Papa gave Miss Moore the information she asked for.

When it came to the birth date, she stopped. "She can't start school yet, she's only five years old."

Papa replied, "She'll be six in November. Why don't you just give her a try? If she can't make it, she can come home." Not really convinced, she let me stay.

Miss Moore was a no nonsense teacher, who knew how to maintain discipline, and how to give children a solid basis in reading, writing, and arithmetic! Those were the days when no whispering or talking was allowed. Chewing gum in school resulted in having to go to the front and spit it out in the wastebasket.

One day I learned that rules were meant to be obeyed. "Alcyon, you will stay in past your time to leave for one hour." I was devastated, sitting alone at my desk with only the older students.

In a room of six grades there was the advantage of hearing the other grades recite, and watching them at the board. Miss Moore let me take the first and second grades that year, and I started the third grade the next fall. Quentin and I walked to school together, along with another neighbor girl, Virginia Stoddard.

I especially liked the spelldowns, and the times when she sent my class to the board for arithmetic. She would give us problems in addition and subtraction and at the word, "Go!" we would start writing furiously. The idea was to be the first one to turn around with the correct answer.

Recently I found a letter that Miss Moore wrote to me from her retirement home. It was after my book, *A Brand From the Burning* came out. It was quite a long letter. Thankfully, she only seemed to remember the positive things about me as a student.

"Do you remember that you entered school at the age of five? I protested, but lost out. Just one other child did I protestingly take in at five years. Her name was Ethel Numbers, a little first grader at the normal school in South Lancaster. She is now Mrs. G. A. Coon, the one who writes for the *Review*, and whose husband is such a wonderful evangelist."

I was happy for the opportunity to visit Miss Moore and to thank her for the good foundation she gave me in school.

"You know," I told her, "when we went as missionaries to Guatemala I had to teach my two little children at home. I went back, over and over again, to the days when I sat in your classroom. I used the same methods you had used."

She just smiled, but her eyes misted. Her life had been her school children.

Chapter 15

The New Baby

It was the age of innocence for children. Nothing was said to us about the new baby Mama was expecting. I took my mother's increased size as something normal. One evening she was eating with her plate on her stomach. I thought that was really interesting. I pushed back and tried to stick my stomach out far enough, but it didn't work! It did furnish a reason for the rest of the family to laugh at my expense.

But it wasn't long until I woke up one morning, with Papa telling me to come and see something. "You have a new baby brother!"

I was enthralled. His name was Wayne. I thought he was the most beautiful baby I had ever seen. I went to school that day, rushing up to the teacher, "Miss Moore! I have a new baby brother. He's just about this long!" And I showed her with my hands about a foot apart.

I was six when Wayne was born, and it wasn't long until Mama let me help her with the baby. I could sit and rock him to sleep with a pillow under my arm for support. I learned to sing the Rock-a-Bye-Baby song. My mother already had some sewing customers, and, as the baby grew, it was my job to watch him and to rock him for his nap.

By the time Wayne was walking, we had moved into a house only two blocks from the church. We could go home for lunch. When school was out in the afternoon, I would run home. By then my mother had many customers. It was the middle of the Great Depression, and my parents were struggling.

I was learning to be my mother's right hand helper. Although Wayne was almost too heavy for me to carry, I was his nursemaid, watching him when he played outside, and rocking him to sleep for his nap. One afternoon. I asked Mama, "Can I go to Alicia's for a little while?" She lived in the next block.

"Yes, you can go for a little while, but get Wayne to sleep first. I have to finish this dress by tomorrow."

I put a pillow under my arm and started rocking the little toddler. Every time he fell asleep I would try to put him down. But he would wake up. Then I would have to go back to the rocker. Finally, I tiptoed with him into the bedroom and he stayed asleep. I ran out the front door and up the street. But, I heard my mother calling. Looking around I saw she was pointing to the little rascal toddling after me. I had to go back and rock some more.

One day when I came home from school, I saw a car out front. It was a sedan, the square black cars of that vintage. When I went in the door, I saw an older, heavy-set lady sitting on a chair near the door. She said, "Oh, this must be Alcyon!"

Seeing the question in my eyes, my mother came to introduce me. "This is your grandma, Grandma Johnson."

Then I knew that it was Mama's mother. I had heard all about her. My mother looked forward to letters from her. But no one else could read them, because they were in Swedish. Grandma took me on her lap, and I saw that she was a jolly, loving Grandma. Her face was round and pleasant, her hair drawn up to a bun on top of her head, and she wore gold-rimmed glasses.

Soon I met my Grandfather Johnson, too. He was retired after being an Adventist minister for many years. In the early days in Minnesota, he was the conference president for the Swedish Conference. Grandma and Grandpa spoke good English, but with a definite Swedish accent. It was the first time we had ever seen our mother's parents. They had lived in Canada, too far away, and it was too expensive for Mama to take us home.

Grandpa Johnson had just purchased his first car, and he wanted to take us for a ride. I sensed, at that age, that he had just learned to drive. Papa and Quentin sat in the front seat with Grandpa, and Grandma, Mama, Wayne and I sat in the back. The seat was really too crowded for four people, so I stood part of the time. It seemed like Grandpa drove fast, the same speed no matter what the roads were like. I was frightened.

Grandma sensed my fear and said, "Don't worry, Alcyon. We are safe. Just sit down and relax!"

From then on, when my mother translated Grandma Johnson's letters, I had a picture of her as that sweet, loving Grandma who held me on her lap.

Ever since coming to Oregon, my parents had gone to every function of the church. Even when we lived farther away our whole family dressed up on Wednesday evening and walked to prayer meeting. We always sat half way back on the right side. Someone must have learned that Mama was a musician, because she soon became the church pianist, and played for every function.

I have never known anyone who was more enthralled with music than my father. As soon as they purchased the first piano, even before I started school, my mother bought the John Williams first grade piano book. Quentin and I both started lessons and she was our teacher. In our family, piano practice was just the same as going to school. You did it, no questions asked. We were supposed to practice an hour a day in the winter and two hours in the summer.

I remonstrated. "Other kids get a vacation from piano practice in the summer."

"That doesn't make sense," Papa informed me. "You have more time in the summer."

Later on, when Mama was too busy, and felt we would do better with a regular teacher, they found one for us. Mandatory practice was a more serious situation than ever. During those depression years, when it was a struggle to pay the rent and keep food on the table, Papa wasn't about to let money spent on lessons go to waste.

They got the idea that Quentin and I should play piano duets. I played the top part, and he the bottom. By then he was old enough to discover how much fun it was to tease me. He would deliberately slow down and speed up, trying to get me off as we played our duets. I would cry, "Mama, make Quentin stop that!"

We knew that failure to do our practicing brought punishment. Sometimes we procrastinated and were still outdoors playing when we saw Papa coming down the street. We both raced to reach the piano first. Sometimes Quentin was trying to push off the bench.

The serious effort our parents made to give us music was something I have thanked them for over and over. Music has been such an important part of my life. Neither they nor I could know that I would be playing for evangelistic meetings someday with my pastor husband leading the music.

Chapter 16

The Pink Organza

"Mama, the spring program will be in two weeks." I came home from school with the news.

"Well, I suppose that means we need a new dress. Is that what you are thinking?" Mama asked with a smile.

She always made me a new dress for the winter and spring programs. But we didn't go to town and buy material. We looked in the trunk of dresses that her customers had given her. My violin teacher, a young Jewish woman, had Mom make all her concert dresses. There was one special one I had my heart set on. It was a beautiful pink organza with hemstitched narrow ruffles all the way down the skirt.

"I suppose you are thinking of that pink ruffled dress of Miss Levy's," Mom said.

"Oh yes!" My eyes lit up. "Could we make it from that one?"

"Yes," she smiled, "I think that is the right material for a spring program," and we began planning the dress. "I suppose you want to use all those ruffles down the skirt."

Even though we were poor, Mama saw to it that we were always dressed well. Her faithful Singer would be put to work.

I had looked at that pink dress many times, hoping that it would someday be used for a new dress for me. I was elated and could just picture myself in that illusion of pink ruffles marching up on the platform.

The next day after school, she brought out the pink dress and I helped her rip out the old seams. It took several days. Finally we had decided on the design. Mama didn't need a pattern. She could copy anything and make up her own patterns.

From then on, every day I rushed home to see how my dress was coming along. I was willing to do anything to help her if she would just work on my dress. Finally, this most beautiful dress I had ever seen hung in the closet waiting for the evening of the program.

But, horror of horrors, the last day of practice, the teacher of the upper grade room, Mrs. Beers, who was also the principal, came into our room to make an announcement.

"We know there may be some students whose parents can't afford new dresses or new suits, so we have decided that everyone shall come in their school clothes."

My heart sank! What would I do? My dress was all finished. My mother had worked long hours, and I had counted the days.

The disappointment and the struggle in my mind were fierce. Shall I tell Mama or not? I knew that if my mother heard about it, or asked me, I would have to tell the truth. But if I didn't say anything, she would never know. Right or wrong, pride won out. It didn't seem to worry me at all that I might be the only one dressed up.

That evening, when I walked down to the church I felt as light as a bird. I had never had such a beautiful dress. I didn't even look at how the others were dressed. I think my mother did say something about wondering why other mothers wouldn't be sure their child was well dressed. But nothing was said to me at home.

However, the next Monday, Mrs. Beers called me into her room. She was not smiling, nor was she very friendly. "Alcyon, did you hear the announcement I made about what to wear at the program?"

I hung my head. "Yes." I had nothing more to say.

"Did you tell your mother?"

"No."

"Why didn't you tell her?"

"I guess it was because she had already made my dress, and I wanted to wear it."

"That's all. You may go now. I will discuss this with your teacher, and we'll decide on your punishment."

I walked out soberly. I had no idea what the punishment would be, but, by the look on her face, I was afraid it might be pretty bad. Also, I knew that if my father heard about it, he would take a pretty dim view of the situation, and there would probably be more than one punishment. However, I still said nothing to anyone. I kept waiting to hear my doom, but day after day went by, and no one said anything more. The secret was mine until years later when I told my mother.

She was pretty shocked, but by then, enough time had gone by, she could laugh about it.

Once while visiting Miss Moore at The Retirement Village in Portland we reminisced over my old school days. When we talked about the dress problem, I asked her why I was never punished.

She laughed. "I just didn't think it was a good idea to make the children wear their old clothes in the first place. I remember you always had quite a bit of spunk."

But there was another time I didn't bring up to her. When I was in the sixth grade, my seat was the last one in the row. There was a boy on each side, also the last ones on their rows. One was Dwight and the other was Harold. It seems that I was old enough to have a childhood sweetheart, or at least I thought I was. Harold was my favorite, and we exchanged notes, but that was all. I liked to draw, and one day I drew a caricature of a boy and girl, with their arms outstretched around each other. I put my name under the girl and his under the boy.

Since I knew that my father didn't think it was appropriate for anyone my age to be looking at the boys, I threw all of Harold's notes in Mill Creek on the way home. Unfortunately, he didn't do the same. Some time later, my preferences went across the aisle the other way toward Dwight. Harold was not happy about that.

During recess one day, Miss Moore motioned to me, "Alcyon, come with me. We are going for a walk."

She led me up to the corner and around the block. Out of sight of the school, she pulled out that dreadful note with the picture on it and showed it to me. "Have you seen this before?"

I had no answer, just hung my head. She didn't say anything more.

Then, in a lighter tone, she said, "Let this be a lesson to you. Don't put things on paper that you might be ashamed of." The lesson was well taken.

Chapter 17

A Little Girl's Prayer

One day when Miss Levy came for a fitting for a dress, she brought a large package and handed it to me.

When I opened it, I was speechless. " Is this for me?"

It was a beautiful big doll, with long hair, a china face and jointed arms and legs. It had been hers as a child. It must have been expensive. I treasured that doll, but one day she met with a catastrophe. She fell and her beautiful china face was broken in several pieces.

I was brokenhearted, but Mama said, "Don't worry, dear. We'll buy some special glue, and I'll help you put the pieces back together. Let's keep the pieces in a special place."

The doll and the pieces were put in a box in the basement. Finally, Mama was ready to glue the doll's face back together. "Go and get your doll, Alcyon, and be sure you get all the pieces."

As she was placing the pieces together, ready to glue them, she exclaimed, "There's a piece missing, and it's the one right in her forehead!"

I ran back down to the basement to look again, but I couldn't find it. Mama went to look too, but that little triangular piece for the forehead was nowhere to be found.

She tried to assure me, "It will probably show up. We'll just put dolly in a safe place until we find it." And she went back to her sewing.

I sat out on the front step, mourning about my poor dolly. But then I remembered that I had been taught, "Jesus hears every prayer." *Would Jesus care about my dolly?* I turned around and knelt right there on the front steps.

"Dear Jesus, You must know what happened to that piece. Please help me to find it!"

And I ran down the basement steps again. Right there on the floor, in plain sight, was the lost piece. I grabbed it up and ran breathlessly up to my mother. "Mama! I prayed, and Jesus helped me to find the lost piece. Look, here it is!"

The doll's face was put together, but most importantly, I learned a lesson in faith. No matter how small or unimportant our requests are, Jesus always hears us. It was the first prayer I remember that God answered to bolster my childish faith, but not the last. Remembering that experience today, I wonder if God was already planning the biggest challenge of my life to my faith.

Chapter 18

Christmas Surprise

All during the depression years, our family, along with most other families, struggled. The little money that came in had to be used for the barest necessities. For Christmas there would be some homemade candy, maybe an orange apiece, and that might be all.

The year that Quentin was ten and I was eight, we had been asking for roller skates. "Everyone at school is getting them," we urged.

Papa loved to get things for his family, but he knew it would be difficult this year. "I wish we could buy you skates, but it is more important that we eat."

Papa's brother from Falls City was cutting Christmas trees in the woods above the little town and bringing them to Salem to sell. Quentin and I helped sell the trees. The night before Christmas Eve we were out in the rain dragging the smaller trees up to people's doors until suppertime. Our uncle must have had some left over and told Papa we could have the money we got out of them. At least we had a tree for our house.

Mama helped us decorate it in high spirits, bringing out a few little bells and trinkets she had to hang on the tree. We made popcorn to string around it. When it was all finished we stood back, our eyes shining. It was beautiful to us. Somehow, some packages appeared under the tree. We could hardly wait. Christmas eve, after our supper, Papa announced, "I think it is time to celebrate Christmas."

We all gathered around in the living room where our tree stood in the corner. Papa had built a fire in the fireplace, and a big pan of apples from the basement sat on a table. There was the telling of the Christmas story and some carols with Mama at the piano.

Then Papa said, "It's time to open the presents." First we received the treats of candy and fruit. Then I found a package with a new dress Mama had made, and Quentin unwrapped a shirt.

We thought that was all, but then Papa said, "You'd better look back behind the tree."

There were two more packages, one for Quentin and one for me. Quentin succeeded in getting his unwrapped first. "Oh! Look! Skates!"

And soon I had my package open, too, and I squealed with joy. "Me, too. I have skates too! Look, my skates have black straps and Quentin's have brown straps!" When the excitement about the skates had died down, Mama went in the bedroom and pulled out a little red wagon. Wayne's eyes grew big and he toddled over to have a look. Quentin put him in the wagon and pulled him around the room. We were almost as excited about Wayne's wagon as our skates.

Even though it was cold and dark outside, we insisted on trying them out on the sidewalk in front of our house. We must have learned on someone else's skates, because we both skated down to the corner and back.

I am sure that our parents did without something to make that Christmas so special for us. And, actually, it was one of the best in my memory.

That next summer Wayne played out in the front yard with his little red wagon. He sometimes left it out there over night. No one seemed to worry about thieving in our neighborhood. One morning when Wayne went out to play, his wagon was gone. Quentin and I searched around the whole neighborhood, but it was nowhere to be found.

Some time later we were playing in the yard of some friends from school, several blocks from our house. Quentin called my attention to a red wagon in the yard. "Look, Alcyon, that looks like Wayne's wagon!" We looked closer. "It is his! See right here where we scratched in his name!"

I asked one of the girls. "Where did you get that wagon? It is my little brother's. He lost it."

"No, that belongs to my little nephew. My brother, Dick, gave it to him." We knew that her brother, Dick, a young teenager, was known as a wild boy.

Quentin and I went to the house and called their mother. "This little wagon belongs to our little brother. Someone took it off of our front yard. See, there is his name."

The woman scowled at us, "That is not your wagon. You kids just run on home."

The wagon was never returned, and years later we saw in the paper where Dick had helped rob a bank in Silverton and killed someone. He ended up in the penitentiary. It taught us how little things can ruin a life.

Chapter 19

Baby Sister

Whenever people ask me how I happened to get involved in International Children's Care, I have to tell them that it goes back a long way to my childhood.

In good weather I would rush home from school to find the newspaper on the front porch. Without even going inside first, I would open to the page where the cartoons were, and spread the pages out on the porch. There was only one that interested me.

I couldn't wait every day to find out what was happening to Little Annie Rooney. It was the continued story of a little orphan girl, who lived in a large typical orphanage of those times. The director was a tall, angular woman, Miss Meany, with a perpetual scowl on her face, who ruled with an iron hand. For some reason she picked on Annie, and the little girl lived in fear and was subjected to all kinds of punishment.

I told my parents, "When I grow up I would like to have an orphanage, but a different kind. I would like to have a place where children are happy and loved like in a real home." I didn't have any idea of how that could be done, just that it needed to be done.

When I was ten Mama was expecting another baby. By then I understood what was going to happen, and couldn't wait. Besides helping care for Wayne, I loved to play with dolls. Now, there would be a real live doll, and Mama promised that I could help her take care of this new baby.

We had moved to a larger house with an upstairs, where the bedrooms were. One night Quentin and I were sent to bed early. We knew that something was happening downstairs. We would slip down the stairs part way and try to find out what was going on. But Papa caught us and made it clear we should go to bed and stay.

The next morning he came to tell us, "You have a new baby sister. You can come down and see her."

"Oh! She is beautiful! Can I hold her?" I cried.

Papa smiled. "She's pretty new and little. Later on you can hold her."

I had prayed for a sister because I already had a little brother. I dearly loved these younger siblings. My mother involved me so much in their care that, years later, when I had children of my own, I felt confident and experienced.

We had a family council to choose a name. My father had this penchant for unusual names, and they named her, La Breta. She became the pet of the family, and I took her on as my special charge, whenever Mama would let me. As I grew a little older, people considered me a responsible baby sitter, and I earned as much as fifty cents for a whole evening!

My mother had a talent for enlisting my help without making it drudgery. She would say, "I need you, Alcyon. Can you help me?"

I never remember her telling me I had to do certain chores, but she let me know that I was her right hand, and she was liberal with the credit she gave me. I loved to work with her. She was cheerful and happy and made every job a challenge for me to do my best.

I give Mama the credit for teaching me to find pleasure and pride in my work. The lessons I learned from her, her special talent in caring for babies, and her efficiency in every thing she did have been valuable to me all through my life. But they have been especially valuable in my life as a missionary, and as the director of a program for homeless children.

Chapter 20

Danger At The River

The summer I was ten, my aunt invited me to stay with them at camp meeting at Gladstone. We had always only been able to go on Sabbaths. This was a special treat for me. I loved the meetings at the Junior tent. There were special speakers, missionaries like Eric B. Hare. There was Arthur Maxwell, whose books I loved. Also, there were special activities.

On hot days, the juniors were taken down to the nearby Clackamas River to swim. There were counselors and older young people to take care of us. My cousin, Ruth, from Falls City, and I went together. She could swim and I was learning, but I was always careful to stay where my feet could touch the bottom.

It was a wonderful time, these junior age children playing, shouting, and enjoying the cool water on the hot day. We were playing off a beach where the depth was gradual. Nearby, was a train trestle, and near it was what was called, The Rocks. We were kept away from that, as it was the favorite diving place into a fifty-foot pool.

Ruth and I were swimming short lengths in the shallow water when, suddenly, her foot hit my leg just enough to push me into an undertow. Soon, I found I couldn't touch bottom, and I was heading out to the deep pool. I tried to swim but my feet were caught in the undertow, and I began to sink.

"Help! Help!" I cried.

Unfortunately, a train was going over the trestle, and my cries for help could not be heard. When I tried to cry I would go under and get my mouth full of water. I went under twice. I was panic stricken as my eyes looked toward the rocks.

Just then, I saw a young man dive in. He swiftly swam to me. And I didn't offer any resistance. He caught me under the chin and swam for the shore.

The party was over for that day! The leaders of the group all gathered around as they carried me up on the beach and began to work, putting my head down and getting the water out of me.

They ordered everyone out of the water and took us back to the campgrounds. That evening at the adult meeting, an announcement was made about the near drowning. The trips to the river for the juniors were over for that year.

I learned the name of the young man who rescued me, and I would never forget his face. He was David Parker. Years later, when we were home on furlough, we were eating in the cafeteria of the Portland Sanitarium. Looking over to one of the nearby tables, I saw a familiar face. I went over and asked, "Would you happen to be David Parker?"

"Yes," he answered, with a question in his eyes.

"Do you remember rescuing a junior girl from the Clackamas River?"

"I certainly do! Are you that girl?"

"I am, and I'm not sure I ever thanked you for saving my life that day." We continued talking as he told me his version of that harrowing experience.

One evening recently at our campfire in the North Cascades, Ken and I were rehearsing God's providences in our lives. I remembered that day that could have been my last on earth.

"I am sure that my guardian angel caused Dave to look my direction, just in time. Could it possibly be that God already had His plan made for my life?"

"I am sure that is true," Ken replied. "And I am equally sure that He is the one that gave you to me for a wife!"

Chapter 21

His Own Pony

Just over the mountains at a ranch in Madras, called **The Lone Juniper Farm**, the Fleck family was arriving, bringing Kenneth home from his first year at Columbia Academy.

"I can hardly wait to see Rover," Kenneth said as they neared Madras

"I'm sure he will be glad to see you, too," his father assured him. "He moped around for quite awhile after you left."

As they drove up the last hill where they could see the Juniper Tree in the distance, the boy's heart leaped. This was home! He couldn't wait to take Rover and strike out across the hills. There was such a sense of freedom.

Rover was there to meet him, and nearly went wild in his joy to see his young master.

"Good boy, Rover! I am so glad to see you!" The boy had Rover enveloped in a big hug, and Rover was whining and licking Kenneth's face in his excitement.

When the family gathered around the table that evening, James suggested, "Why don't you offer the blessing tonight, Kenneth? It is a good feeling to have our family all together again here in our own home."

While they were eating, his father turned to the boy. "You know, Son, while you were gone I always had to hire another man to help me, or do all the farm work myself. But you are big and strong. From now on, we'll work together. You will take the place of a hired man. How does that sound?"

"I'd like that, Papa. I know how to do lots of things. I've already driven the teams. You just tell me what my jobs are."

"When you finish eating, come out to the barn to see something," James told him.

Kenneth didn't linger over his food! When he went out to the barnyard, he saw a young pony. "Where did he come from?" he asked, walking up to the pony.

"I thought it was time you had your own horse," his father said. "He's yours."

"Mine? Really! I can't believe it! I'll call him, Billy"

The rest of the family had followed them out to see Kenneth meet his new pony. His father assured him, "He's broken for riding. You can jump on him."

Kenneth grabbed a bridle and soon he was on Billy's back. He took a turn up the road. When he came back, the family was still there. "I think he knows me already," he shouted.

There were chores to be done before breakfast to prepare for the days work in the field. After breakfast, that first workday, the family gathered for worship. Then Kenneth and James grabbed their hats, gloves, and jackets, and left for the barn. "You can drive the four horse team," his father said. "I'll take the six horse team." Kenneth followed his father's team with his four horses abreast. They headed for the field that they would work and prepare for the summer fallow.

He had driven the team before, during harvest, and felt like a grown man that day. They drove their teams side by side, ten horses wide, around and around the field. At noon, James called a halt. "I see the sun is straight up. We'll give the horses a rest while we go for dinner."

"That's a good idea!" Kenneth replied. "It seems like quite a while since breakfast."

When they finished eating, it was back to the field, continuing round and round the fields until time for supper.

When they drove the teams back to the barn for the night, each horse knew his own stall, and would walk right in, glad for the grain and hay waiting for him. James taught his son to take good care of the horses and to always be kind to their animals.

When Sabbath came, they gathered for their Home Sabbath School. Kenneth and Jean traded off being superintendent, Sabbath School Secretary and the one to give the mission talk. It was out of the mission quarterly sent to them in the mail each quarter. They all took turns teaching the lesson. Those home Sabbath Schools had a strong influence on Kenneth and Jean that they would always remember.

Chapter 22

Goodbye Lone Juniper Farm

James was keeping a close eye on the wheat fields. He confided to Ida one morning when he came in for breakfast, "Well, the crop looks about normal, not great, but about as well as we usually do in this area."

By then he had acquired an old John Deere tractor and was farming about 1200 acres. They were making a living, but working hard to do it. He knew they would never get rich on that farm, that is as long as it was dry farming. There was talk of irrigation coming to that area, but no one knew when that might happen.

It wasn't just the quality of their soil that concerned Ida and James. Their children were growing up. They hated to send Kenneth so far away to school, and Jean was still in the country school. She had to walk two and a quarter miles through the barren countryside alone every day.

"I just wish we could live down in the valley, closer to Meadow Glade," Ida said.

"I've been thinking about that, too." James added. "Maybe we should pursue some other options."

After discussing different ideas, and praying about it, they decided to make plans toward a move closer to Meadow Glade and discussed it with the children.

One day James talked to Kenneth. "You know we haven't been sure we could afford to send you back to Columbia this year. Would you be disappointed to stay out of school this year and help me on the farm, while we arrange to move closer to Meadow Glade?"

Kenneth was quick to reply. "No, Papa. I don't mind staying home this year. I would lots rather go to school down there if you lived closer so I could go home more often. I like being here on the farm. And I have Billy and Rover."

When they were in Meadow Glade to bring Kenneth home, James had done some inquiring about possibilities. He had a friend there, whose brother lived in Longview. "I've heard there is a dairy farm that might be available out by the Weyerhaeuser Mill," the man told him.

That fall, when the harvest was finished, and James felt he could be gone for a few days he told Ida, "I think I should make a trip to Meadow Glade. I can do some serious inquiring, and possibly find out about that farm in Longview."

Ida was happy. "That's a good idea. This is a good time to go. Kenneth can handle the milking and necessary chores while you are gone."

The family was eager to know what James found out on his trip. When he returned they couldn't wait to hear. "Tell us, Papa! Are we going to move?"

He was smiling. "Yep, it looks like we may be dairy farmers. I have an option to rent the farm in Longview."

Ida couldn't wait to hear more. "Tell us all about it!"

"There are about 60 acres. It is near the Columbia River, just across the road from the big Weyerhaeuser Mill. There is a barn with a herd of cows already milking."

"How about a house?" Ida urged.

"Well, there's an old house. It isn't much, but I guess it will do for a while. One big problem is that there is no good well on the place. We will have to haul our water for the house from town."

Ida was not daunted. "We'll make do somehow. The important thing is to live where we will be closer to Columbia Academy, and a Christian school for Jean. I'm sure there will be a church in Longview. Just imagine! Having a church to go to every Sabbath!"

As soon as he could make the financial arrangements with the owner, and find a solution for the Lone Juniper Farm, they made definite plans for the move the next summer.

Before harvest time, James had finalized on renting the Longview farm. The busy days of harvest went by quickly, and the day was set when they would leave the Lone Juniper Farm and head toward the new venture of operating a dairy farm in Longview.

Kenneth was concerned,

"What about Billy?"

"Don't worry, Son, Billy will come to Longview, as well as both dogs. Besides Rover, another dog, Ring, had come while Kenneth was away at school.

Billy and Kenneth had become close friends. One day he rode up to the front gate and called his mother. "Come and see something!"

When she came out on the front porch, the boy whistled to Rover. "Come on, Rover!" he called, patting Billy's back. Rover gave one leap and landed behind Kenneth and they galloped off together.

"What that boy won't think of!" she said, going back into the house.

Rover liked to ride behind Kenneth, but Billy didn't always like it, especially when Rover dug his claws into his back. Kenneth would hang on, but sometimes Rover got bucked off.

Moving day came. The truck was loaded, and the Fleck family was ready to leave for the trip to Longview. There was sadness mixed with the anticipation of the new home. The car pulled out, with the truck following behind. At the top of the hill, they took one last look. Kenneth voiced the feelings of them all. "Goodbye, Lone Juniper Farm. We'll never forget you."

Chapter 23

Back in School

"There's our new farm!" James pointed to the land off to his right as he neared the lane that would lead into the new farm.

"Hey! There are some cows out there in the field! Will they be ours?" Kenneth asked.

"They probably are. The cows go with the place." James led the way into the lane, with the truck following behind.

When Ida walked into the house, she looked all around, noticing the cobwebs, the floors that needed scrubbing, and walls that needed fresh paint. "Well," she began, "I guess our work is cut out for us. This house needs help! But at least we are here, and we'll soon make it seem like home."

It was the last day of August, Jean's birthday. "This will probably be a birthday you won't forget, Jean," her father told her with a smile.

They were a busy family for the next few weeks. Kenneth helped his father to clean up the barn, milk the new cows, check on all the fences, and get settled into working a dairy farm. But he didn't have long to help, as school would be starting soon.

Aunt Mamie and her husband, Uncle Tom, with their children had finished the house they were building on their own acreage. The attic was still unfinished, but Kenneth would be living with them while attending

Columbia Academy. His bed was located under the eaves, with only the shingles between him and the night air. In return for his board and room, he would be helping around the place, milking the cow, and wherever he was needed. Their youngest, Ida Belva, was still a baby in diapers. Washing diapers was one of the chores that had to be done every day, and Kenneth was initiated into that rather unpleasant process.

The family walked the half-mile or so to church on Sabbaths. Ida Belva had to be carried. "Here, Kenneth, carry her for me for awhile," Aunt Mamie would say.

He loved little Ida Belva, and thought she was beautiful. But he didn't really want the fellows to see him carrying her. When they neared the church, he would hand her back to her mother.

Kenneth was involved in all of the activities of the school, even though he didn't live on campus. He was soon back as part of the male quartet. When the school was asked to give programs in nearby churches, the quartet usually furnished the music.

Vespers was a special time. His heart was stirred with the inspiring programs and talks from faculty or visitors. When it came time for the testimonies, many students stood to tell of their desires to follow Jesus or to tell of some experience. Kenneth had a hard time getting to his feet at first, but he really wanted to express the feelings that stirred in his heart.

He finally got the courage to stand and say a few words. After that it wasn't so hard. *If I ever think of being a minister, I'll have to learn to talk up in front*, he would tell himself. *It's a little different talking in front of all these students than in my house on the farm.*

Although there had never been a definite time when he decided, "Yes, I'm going to be a minister," somehow he always felt that people expected that of him, and that was probably what he would do.

Kenneth became a favorite among his classmates. He had lots of friends, both girls and boys.

During his junior year, he had a friend, Dorothy, a girl who worked at his Uncle Elmer's while attending school. Although it was against the rules, he walked her home one evening after the vesper service. Instead of going directly to the house, they walked on up the road, and then back. He never knew who saw them and reported it to the principal. The next Sunday he spent all day out on the stump pile, digging out stumps.

When I asked him if he always had a girl friend, he admitted, "Yes, I guess I always liked one special girl better, but they changed fairly often!"

As soon as school closed for the year, Ken's parents came to visit Grandma and Aunt Mamie's. "Are you ready to go home for the summer?" his father asked.

"Yes, I've been looking forward to spending the summer on the new farm."

"Well, we can use your help. Milking almost 30 cows morning and night is a big job. Mama helps me some times."

"She won't have to milk when I am home," the young man asserted.

The folks had done a lot to the place during the last year. The old house looked like home. There was an attic with two areas. Ken's bed was at one end, and the extra bed that Grandma Lashier used when she visited them was at the other end.

That summer went by fast. The Fleck family settled into their new home, and they had a church at last.

Whither Thou Goest

Kenneth worked with his father on the farm. Their situation began to look up.

Chapter 24

Ken Graduates

The Sunday morning they were to take Kenneth back to school, he and his father were up early to get the milking done. They would need to take the milk to the creamery and bring the water back. While Ida and Jean were putting breakfast on the table, the men were loading Kenneth's suitcases that were already on the back porch. The whole family would be going along.

Arriving at Aunt Mamie's she was ready for them. "Just put your things upstairs, Kenneth. You know where your room is."

"Right, up in the attic!" It didn't take long for the seventeen-year-old to settle in to his little corner up under the eaves.

Later Kenneth and his father went to the business office to make financial arrangements for Kenneth's tuition. He realized that his parents were making a sacrifice to keep him in a Christian school, and he determined to make them proud of him. "Thanks a lot, Papa, for all you are doing for me. I feel guilty to not stay home and help you on the farm."

His father gave him a hug. "Just do your best, Son. We'll be praying for you. We'd best be getting back. Mom and I need to be heading out to be home in time for the milking."

After telling his family goodbye from Grandma's house, Kenneth walked on over to Aunt Mamie's place.

Tomorrow would be the first day of his senior school year.

Uncle Elmer's youngest son, Wendell, was a year behind Kenneth in school. He lived the other direction from the school, but they saw each other whenever they could and were close friends. Wendell had the same friendly personality as Kenneth and was equally well liked.

That year Wendell was elected student body president and Kenneth was treasurer. Even in later years, people thought of them as brothers. Their aptitudes were different. Kenneth was involved in music activities, and developed more and more into a tenor soloist. Wendell was known for his business leanings.

Evern Budd, Emmett Roderick, and Ernie Cornelius were Kenneth's friends all through academy. Another friend through his academy and college years was George Chalker. Their friendship was based largely on their mutual interest in music. They both had good voices, and were involved in the musical activities. Both aspired to the ministry and especially to singing evangelism.

The seniors were often involved in the missionary activities, going to surrounding churches on Sabbath. There was a tradition for Columbia Academy and a sister Academy, Laurelwood, to exchange programs. During this senior year, Kenneth and George were in the group who gave the program at Laurelwood.

On Sabbath afternoon, George visited Eugene Sample, a student at Laurelwood.

"Did you know that my grandmother married your great-grandfather, Elder Andrew Stover after they both lost their spouses?" George asked.

Eugene was surprised. "No, I hadn't heard that."

George told Kenneth that evening; "I met Eugene's cousin today. Her name is Alcyon Logan, from Salem. She is a freshman. Eugene told me that she is musical, plays both the piano and violin. She was surprised when Eugene told her I was a relative." Neither of them could have imagined the significance of that encounter with the freshman girl.

The last weeks before graduation at Columbia Academy were busy ones, but amidst the last senior events, the finals and the graduation plans, most of the graduates were wondering what the future would hold. Tuition with board and room in the dormitory was only $25 per month, but many of the students had a hard time paying their bill, Kenneth included. He knew and his parents knew that he must find a way to go on to college. Kenneth understood his parent's situation and agreed to a year at home, helping on the dairy farm.

Graduation day came, a day the seniors had anticipated for four years. But it was also a sad day of parting with friends, knowing that many of them would be heading down different paths. When Kenneth's bags were in the car, ready to leave for Longview, he told Aunt Mamie and her family goodbye. "Thank you, Aunt Mamie, for making room for me in your home. I feel like one of the family."

When he told Wendell goodbye, they promised to keep in touch and make their plans for the following year at Walla Walla.

That night, at home in his attic bedroom, Kenneth thought back on his academy years. They were good years, filled with many friends and memories that would be with him the rest of his life. But now, he must set his face toward the future, one that held many unknowns, but also many possibilities. He little realized all that his Father in Heaven had in store for him.

Chapter 25

"What Religion?"

Because of a serious problem with a teacher that had to be fired from the upper grades in our Salem church school, my parents sent me to the public Junior High for my eighth grade. It was a drastic change from our little private school but I adjusted. Everything went well for me, except in the Home Economics class.

The teacher was a single woman who shouted her orders and didn't mind embarrassing a student. We all had individual cooking units around the room, and she stood in the middle, giving orders. We were to make clam chowder one day. Our family was vegetarian. I had never even tasted meat. The teacher had a rule that you had to at least try everything you made. She watched as everyone around the room took a spoonful of clam chowder, that is everyone but me. I was trembling, but I could not do it. She shouted, "Alcyon! Take a bite!"

Timidly, I answered, "I can't."

"Why not?" she shouted.

"Because I don't eat meat."

"What religion?"

"Seventh-day Adventist," I told her.

"I'll tend to you later."

That night I told my parents about the incident in cooking class. "Do I really have to go to that school?" I asked tearfully. "There is another student, who is the teacher's pet and assistant. She goes to our church. She must not be a vegetarian."

Papa told me, "You did the right thing, Alcyon. We are proud of you. I know it isn't easy, and it was cruel of that teacher to humiliate you in class."

Mom was listening, and was quick to suggest I shouldn't have to take that class.

"Well, this has been a test for her," Papa replied. "But she has shown her character." Then turning to me, he added, "Just go on as if nothing happened. God will be with you. You need to finish the year."

Miss Welch never mentioned the incident to me again, but there was another teacher in that school from our church. She was a kind woman and knew my parents. She called me into her room. "Alcyon, what is the problem between you and Miss Welch? She says you are not cooperative."

With tears I told her of my ordeal in class. She was sympathetic. "Just try to be as respectful as you can," she advised me.

Mama and Papa decided that the next year both Quentin and I should go to Laurelwood Academy, a boarding school near Forest Grove. The Junior High consisted of 7th, 8th, and 9th grades. I finished the 8th grade there.

When the church announced there would be a special event for prospective students at Laurelwood, I came home excited. "Can I go?"

I was 12, and would be 13 in November. Although I was pretty young to go away from home, I came back from that visit bubbling with enthusiasm. "I even found my roommate," I told the family.

That summer was full of plans and preparation. I was in my glory, couldn't wait to go. My parents were not financially able to send us away to school, but they were doing their best. Even with the expenses only $29 per month, and my working almost half of it, they got behind.

My job that year was to wash dishes after every meal. There were three huge metal tubs for dishwashing. One was for the rinse before going into the second, hot sudsy water, and the third was the real hot rinse. I washed the dishes, and put them into the hot rinse. There was a girl at each tub, and we would race to try to get ahead of the next girl. The girl at the rinse tub stacked the dishes for drying. We timed it once and counted the dishes. There were a little more than 600 dishes and it took us 30 minutes.

One weekend Columbia Academy came to give us a program. These were social times when we could get acquainted with the Columbia students. My cousin, Eugene Sample, a junior at Laurelwood, introduced me to a student in their group, a member of their men's quartet.

"This is George Chalker, Alcyon. You remember Great-Grandpa Stover. Remember that he married again after his first wife died? Well, it was George's grandma that he married. We are sort of cousins."

I was interested to hear about that, but didn't give it a lot of thought. Little did I ever dream what the future held for me that would include George and his friend, Kenneth Fleck.

At the end of the school year, my bill wasn't paid; it was a big disappointment when I knew I would have to go to high school. During that year, the Venden Brothers had a citywide campaign. It was during that time that I became acquainted with the girl who became one of my best friends, Enid Venden. Her father was Joe Venden, Dan and Melvin's eldest brother. She was staying with her Uncle Dan while attending school.

That year we moved to a small community about 30 miles from Salem. There was a property for rent that included a natural mineral spring and a large building like a lodge. Papa was enthusiastic. This reminded him of Battle Creek, and it seemed affordable, since it had been empty and the owners were anxious to rent it. The surroundings were wooded. It all seemed ideal as a health retreat.

I was 14 and Quentin 16. By then we had a car, and Quentin had his license. I was overjoyed one day when Papa told me, "We just paid up the Laurelwood bill, and made arrangements for you to go back this year."

"Really? Oh! I am so glad! But what about Quentin?"

"He plans to go to the local high school here. He doesn't enjoy being away at school as much as you do."

Chapter 26

The Banquet

I was thrilled to be back in Laurelwood and was a junior that year. The vesper services were always special to me. I was inspired with the talks, and would always stand at a call, but could never get the courage to give a testimony. I would sit there trying to think what I would say, but by the time I got it figured out, it was over!

It was during that year that I began to think about my future. I knew I wanted to go to college. I even looked in catalogues that showed available Adventist nursing schools. I had wanted to be a missionary ever since the days when I sat in grade school. I loved to listen to mission stories and read mission story books. It seemed like nursing would fit into a mission life the best.

It was a great year for me. I worked hard, but still my folks couldn't keep up with the monthly bill. At the end of the school year, I knew that I wouldn't be able to come back.

Near the end of the summer my father talked to me. "I'm sorry we don't have your bill paid. I know how much you wanted to graduate at Laurelwood."

"I suppose I should plan on going to the high school here," I answered.

"Unless there is some wind-fall, I'm afraid that you will have to. Quentin finished up the year here, and he seemed to think it is a good school."

That fall I enrolled in the local high school as a senior. Although I knew hardly anyone, I soon had some friends. One day I came home with the news, "They asked me to be the pianist for the Glee Club."

"That's good," Mama replied. "It will help to keep you involved in music."

Then one day I came home with more news.

"There was an election for the president of the Girls' Club today, and they made me president."

While my parents seemed happy for me, they may have been concerned with my having so much involvement in the high school activities, but nothing was said.

That small high school had a football team that was making waves. They went on trips to play other teams. Their success was trumpeted locally. One of the star players was a tall, handsome boy named Howard. His parents ran a farm not too far from us. I had only seen him at school but we were friends.

When he went with the team, to play one of their most critical games, I received a card. "We are having a great time, but am thinking about you. Love, Howard."

It was time for another Girls' Club meeting, and the principal approached me. "You know, Alcyon, the club should think of a project for this year."

"I know," I answered. "Do you have any suggestions?"

"I'm sure you and the other girls will think of something," he replied, leaving me wondering what to do.

At the next meeting I had an idea. "You know, girls, our football team has been putting our school on the map this year. What would you think of giving them a banquet?"

"Yes! Yes!" They chorused. "Let's do it!"

The rest of the meeting was spent on plans for the banquet. We organized committees, and I promised to talk to the principal for an appropriate date. We had committees for decorating, for the program, for collecting supplies, and for the menu.

Coming in from school one day I headed for the kitchen where I knew I would find my mother. "Mom! We have our banquet all arranged."

"That's good," she answered. "What are your plans?"

"Different mothers are helping with the dinner. The food committee decided on fried chicken, mashed potatoes and gravy, peas, light buns and apple pie. We have everything arranged for, except the pie. I was hoping you would make the pies for us."

"My, my! That's quite a tall order! How many will you need?" She looked up from the kettle she was stirring on the stove.

"Could you make twenty-five?" I asked, hopefully.

"Twenty-five! I've never made that many pies at one time in my life!"

"I know it's too much to ask, but I would help, and I can get some girls from school to help too."

My mother was such a trouper. I could always count on her. She didn't seem to know how to say "no" to us.

The evening of the banquet arrived. Everyone had done his or her part. The room was decorated in fall colors. Candles lit the tables. There were place cards in front of each plate. Each football player sat with the girl of his choice. I was at the speaker's table with Howard at my side. Speeches were made, the dinner was perfect. The girls who had been chosen to serve did it beautifully.

When it was all over, the principal came to me, "That was a beautiful job, Alcyon. You did something that hasn't been done here before, at least as long as I have been here. I think it might become a tradition. Congratulations!"

All the compliments were exciting for me. I went home that evening with my head in the clouds. But, up in my room that night, lying awake in bed, my thoughts were confused. *I like my friends at this school. It was fun doing the banquet, but I miss my friends at Laurelwood. I miss the Christian atmosphere. I miss the Friday night vespers. I hope that going to high school doesn't change me. I want to go to a Christian college and prepare to be a missionary.* Kneeling by my bed, I prayed for strength to be a Christian no matter where I went.

Chapter 27

The Race

Just a hundred miles to the north in Longview, Kenneth was ready to begin his year helping on the dairy.

That first morning he heard his father call, "Kenneth! Kenneth! It's five o'clock! Time to go milk the cows!"

He hurried into his clothes, and soon Kenneth and his father were out in the barn. As each cow was milked she was turned loose to go out to the pasture. The cans of milk were hauled to the trailer to be taken to the creamery.

While Kenneth was taking the place of a hired man, he found time to study his Bible and read. *If I want to be a minister, I need to be preparing for it*, he thought.

One day when he was sick, he read *Messages to Young People* in one sitting. Another time he read the New Testament in one sitting. Steps to Christ was one of his favorite books, and that year he read it again, underlining all of his favorite quotes.

But life was not all serious. One morning he told his family, "I read that the County Fair is starting next week. There will be a pony race for boys up to 18. I guess that Billy and I would qualify. What do you think?"

"I think you should enter the race," his mother told him. "Billy is a fast pony and you handle him well."

Chuckling, his father added, "Sure, if I was younger I'd get in that race myself."

"You children should have seen your father with his fancy horses when he was courting me!" Ida told them with a sparkle in her eyes.

Jean added her opinion. "We will all go and cheer for you."

The day of the race, Kenneth curried Billy, fed and watered him, then dressed himself like a typical western cowboy.

This race was to be run bareback. He was right in the starting line up, and Billy was prancing around, raring to go. When the flag went down, they were off!

James stood up from his seat on the bleachers, "Go Billy!" he yelled.

The track was dirt, and soon it was hard to distinguish the horses or riders for the dust. Kenneth was giving Billy his head and urging him to put everything he had into it. Soon the dust was so thick, Kenneth could hardly even see if there was someone in front of him. He thought he might be in the lead.

In the spectator's section Jean was yelling, "Go! Billy!

Soon James shouted, "Look! He's coming up. There are just two ahead of him! Can you see, Ida? Is that Kenneth gaining on the first horse?"

"I can't tell. How in the world can those riders see the track for that thick dust?"

Coming in on the final round, Billy was gaining on the fellow in front, who was riding a race type horse. Kenneth thought he was in the lead, but couldn't be sure for the thick dust. He was leaning on Billy's neck. "Go, Billy, go!" he cried into the pony's ear.

As the speeding riders came in on the final round, the horse ahead of Billy crossed the finish line just enough in front of Kenneth and Billy to win first prize.

When they announced the winners, the loud speaker called out, "Second prize goes to Kenneth Fleck on Billy!"

First prize was a 5-gallon can of fly spray, and second prize was a little fat pig! Kenneth managed to trade with the first prize-winner and then handed his father the can of fly spray for the cows.

Chapter 28

The Fire

It was almost time for Kenneth to leave for college. He had already purchased the new clothes they were able to afford. All of the things he would take with him were stacked up in his room in the attic.

Grandma Lashier was visiting them, which she often did. Her room was on the other end of the attic. She had brought quite a suitcase full of clothes and a box or two. As James brought it in from the car for her, she explained, "I don't like to leave anything valuable in my old house. If it caught fire, it would go fast."

Grandma's nephew and Ida's cousin was an interesting family character they called, Uncle Arthur. He had come to visit that day. Ida and Jean had gone shopping, and Kenneth was in the far field raking hay with the horses. There were trees that blocked his view of the house from where he was in the field. All at once he looked toward home. "Could that smoke be coming from our house?"

He dropped the reins and left the horses where they stood in the field and ran to the house. The roof was in flames. Soon James saw it and came running too. Men from the Weyerhaeuser mill came. When Kenneth got there, he found Grandma and Uncle Arthur just pulling the piano out the door. Soon there was lots of help, bringing most of the furniture out and onto the lawn before the fire engulfed the first floor.

The house was a complete loss, and nothing was saved from the attic. Kenneth lost everything except the clothes on his back, and Grandma lost all the things she had brought along for safe keeping!

Ida and Jean arrived home in time to see the house in flames. Ida was inconsolable, and collapsed on the sofa out on the lawn. "What will we ever do now?" she wailed.

Kenneth, as well as others, was trying to comfort his mother. But, what about him? What about his plans for college? It was a catastrophe for the Fleck family, and they wondered how they could survive.

But James was not one to be vanquished. "Don't worry, Ida. God will see us through somehow. No one was hurt. We are all here. Let's thank God for that."

There was a small two-room cabin a little distance down a path in front of the house. It had been used for hired help. When Ida got herself together she realized, "We can move into the cabin. At least we have most of our furniture." After thoroughly cleaning it they found shelter there.

People from the church were kind and helpful. The pastor suggested, "There is this tabernacle that was put up in sections. We are through with it now. Maybe we can arrange with the conference to let you buy it to use what you can for a new house."

The arrangements were made, and eventually another house sat on the same spot as the older one. It didn't have two stories, but there were three small bedrooms, as well as a kitchen, dining room and adjoining living room. There still was no electricity, or running water in the house. Luckily the outhouse didn't burn!

Chapter 29

"What Do You Believe?"

In spite of the tragedy of the fire and losing everything, Kenneth still managed to go to college that year.

"Is that where we have to sleep?" Kenneth asked his cousin, Wendell, looking at the antique leather lounge that folded down to make a bed.

They had found an upstairs apartment they could rent for a reasonable amount. When the two boys tried the lounge the first night, they ended up in a fit of laughter. There was such a sag toward the middle; they had to get in bed at the same time, back to back. The one bedroom was for Mildred, Wendell's older sister, who cooked for them in the small kitchen.

Both boys found work at the College Store. That, along with other little jobs they could find, and the help from home, would get them through the year.

In those days there were two English classes for freshmen, the regular and the bonehead class. Every new student took the examination that decided which class they should be in.

Wendell didn't like English. He preferred math and history. But Kenneth had always excelled in English. He was puzzled when he found himself in the Bonehead class. He didn't know until the end of the quarter that his name had been confused with Wendell's! So Kenneth ended up with a very good foundation in

English, and the teacher wondered what he was doing there!

He chose theology as his major but as he went along, there was a lingering doubt. When he heard the professors talk about the call to the ministry, he wondered when, and if, he really had received that call. College exposed him to new influences, even to some concepts in his classes that were strange and troubling to him. Could it be that he had just simply been programmed to think he should be a minister? How could he know if this was God's plan for him?

In a confidential discussion with one of his friends he asked: "How do you feel about some of the things you see here, such as the swing band, professors drinking coke at the drug store, and some of their jesting? I thought this was a Christian college."

"Frankly, I don't know what to think," his friend confided. "It seems like a different world here. The standards are so different."

"Well," Kenneth went on, "I'm sure it doesn't represent every teacher. I really like Elder Berg's class. It is so spiritual."

"Yes, I feel the same way, but in some of my Bible classes, I'm not sure the professors are even real Adventists."

He tried to put these concerns out of his mind. Kenneth was a social person. He soon made lots of friends. Many of them were discussing their dates for Saturday night. That consisted of going to the school function, whatever that was. Rules were not as strict as at the academy, but there definitely were rules. There were rules about proper conduct with the opposite sex. There were dress codes. You always went to class with shirt and tie. Casual clothes were for recreation and work.

He asked one of his friends, Forrest Roper, a theology student, "Is it really true that there is trouble in the Theology Department?"

"So far, all I really know is what is rumored," he answered. "But I am concerned. It seems that some of the teachers, who have gone to secular universities for their advanced degrees, come back with their faith in the basic doctrines of the Adventist church shaken."

"I have wondered," Kenneth added, "if I was understanding right in some of my classes."

Students were going home to their parents and pastors with questions. It was a time of deep perplexity in the lives of many of the theology students. One day Kenneth went to one of those teachers and asked him a question about his beliefs.

The teacher just looked off into the distance and replied, "Frankly, I don't know just what I believe anymore."

For a young freshman, thinking he would find all his answers at college, this was very confusing. In discussing the problem with other students, his concerns only deepened.

"I think the dean of the Theology Department is almost pro-Catholic in his attitudes," one of his friends said. "I was invited to Dr. Schilling's house. In the basement he has what he calls his sanctuary. He has candles, rich drapery, and decor to resemble a temple. He called it, 'my private sanctuary'."

Behind the scenes the powers that be were investigating the situation. It was earth shaking when the three of the main professors of the Theology Department were dismissed. Even the president of the college was brought down, supposedly for having allowed the situation.

It was a devastating experience for the students, including Ken.

Not long after that, another student said, "I was coming from a Sabbath appointment, and drove by an Episcopalian church on Sabbath. Dr. Schilling was out mowing the lawn with a big cigar in his mouth. I heard that he has taken a position as pastor of that church."

There was need of serious damage control after this destructive episode in the most important department of the college. After all, Walla Walla College was founded to prepare workers and missionaries to help proclaim the gospel to the world. Kenneth was glad when George McCready Price came to help restore the image of the college. He announced very emphatically to the board and to the students, "I want you to know one thing. I'm no heretic! You are going to hear the gospel just like the pioneers preached it!"

Elder J.I. Robison also came later to fill in a vacancy in the department. Those who knew Elder Robison remembered him as a man of unquestionable ethics and character, a true Adventist in every sense of the word.

During this time, many theology students had intense conversations about the problem, and some of them went through a period of questioning in their own minds. Kenneth was among them. "If these men, who have studied the Bible and the Spirit of Prophecy for years are confused about their faith and their beliefs, how can I be sure of anything?"

His second year, Kenneth found a job milking Dr. Reith's cow and doing other chores in exchange for his board and room. In telling me about this he said, "I think it was more of a help to me than I was to them. I still had a job at the store, besides all my classes and college activities."

Miss Ruth Havsted was a voice teacher as well as choir and A Capella Choir director. Being part of the A Capella was a thrill for Kenneth, and he learned a lot about voice training from Miss Havsted. There were trips all over the Northwest to give concerts.

Ken, as I call him, was always called Kenneth by his parents and family. But his young friends called him Kenny, and I first knew him as Kenny. Some of his college friends began to call him Ken, and he liked that.

Chapter 30

A Critical Decision

The next year, the cousins lived in West Hall, an annex to the boy's dormitory. Ken was involved in many activities. He was still a member of the A Capella choir, and a men's quartet. That year his quartet was officially called The College Quartet.

He had a friend, we will call Lee, who was a bright student, a fun person to be with, but who did not have the same goals or standards as Ken. Lee would often ask him to go off campus to some game or other recreation with a group of friends. Little by little, the carefree influence of these friends began to affect Ken's thinking, and soon his grades began to suffer.

One evening Lee told him, "There is a great movie in town. A lot of the guys are going. Why don't you come along?"

"But that's against school rules." He didn't mention that he had never gone to shows.

Lee just laughed, "Don't worry about the rules. When some of us want to go, we just call up the theater and tell them to open the back door for us. No one knows we are there."

Ken tried to beg off, but Lee was insistent, and Ken thought, I guess one time won't hurt. His spiritual decline with the wrong friends was taking its toll. Although they sat in an inconspicuous place near the front, he was shocked to see another theology student in the audience.

While his spiritual condition was in trouble, Ken maintained an outward conformity to the standards of the school and an apparent interest in the spiritual activities. In truth, he was living a double life. In his heart he was miserable, and the struggle between Satan and God raged within him. He began to wonder, *am I studying theology because I was programmed by my parents and teachers in the academy? For that matter, am I an Adventist, simply because I was raised in this church?* He knew that he would have to find answers, and that he could not straddle the fence much longer.

One day Ken stayed in bed because of a sinus infection and headache. It was snowing, and the ground was white. When some of his friends came from eating in the cafeteria he asked them, "What did you have to eat?"

One of them replied, "You should have been there."

"Well, if you'll carry me over there, I'll go!"

In a moment those young college "friends" picked him up in his pajamas, barefooted, and carried him over to the cafeteria that was in the basement of Conard Hall. They went around to the back door and set him down.

When he told me about it, I asked, "How did you get back?"

"I ran through the snow, and hopefully, so fast no one could recognize me!"

No one knew that inside he wasn't quite the same person he appeared to be. He was very jovial, with the "life of the party" personality.

Although the deep questions remained, life went on at school. There were times when he spent time studying and praying, and other times he went along with Lee and some of his friends.

It was nearing the end of the year. Ken and Lee were discussing their future. Lee surprised his friend with the announcement, "Kenny, I've decided to join the Navy Air force."

"Really, tell me more about it."

Lee went on to extol the advantages. There would be free education, a lucrative career and a good retirement. "I won't have to worry about school bills any more."

Ken wanted to know more. "What do you have to do to get in? I might like to look into it. I've thought I would like to be a pilot."

"I'll take you down to the recruiting office, and you can see for yourself," Lee told him.

The next afternoon the two fellows went to town. Ken came home with all the papers, including the forms to fill out. He put them in a drawer. *I'll need to think about this.*

It was a strong temptation, but, in the end, he knew he couldn't do it. At the time, he didn't understand that God had a different plan for his life, something far more rewarding than a life in the navy. God was winning the battle for his soul. It was almost a relief when he told Lee, "I know it would offer a lot, but I guess it isn't for me."

Years later Ken saw Lee, who had retired from the Navy as an Admiral. But he died later with a drinking problem without any hope in God. Ken was thankful for the decision that God helped him make so many years before.

Ken knew that, after his year in the dorm, his account would not be settled in time for the following year. He would be looking forward to, at least, a quarter at home. The pastor of his home church had indicated that he needed a song leader for an evangelistic campaign. Maybe that would be an option.

He was able to help his father with the milking and still help Elder Dickinson with the meetings. He was in charge of the music, and, for the first time, began to do more solos. He also helped with the visitation and Bible studies.

When campmeeting time came, the Flecks had a tent at the grounds at Gladstone Park. Ken and his father still had the milking to do, but arranged to go as much as possible. He had no idea what an impact events at that campmeeting would have on his future.

Chapter 31

Crisis at Campmeeting

At the beginning of that summer when I was sixteen I began to think about campmeeting. When Enid wrote that a lady from her church was looking for someone to share her tent, I asked Mama what she thought.

"I don't know what Papa would say. What would you use for money?"

"I'm thinking of picking berries. There's a field just walking distance from here."

Surprisingly, my father gave his consent. He approved of my friendship with Enid, who would be tenting with her parents. He probably thought that, after my year in public high school, going to campmeeting would be good for me.

Wayne, now ten years old, wanted to go berry picking with me. So, every morning for several weeks we walked to the berry field and worked all day. By the time the berry harvest was over, I had enough saved up. I could hardly wait. Campmeeting began on Wednesday evening. The folks would come on Sabbath.

Enid was already there and she took me to meet Mrs. Currant. Once I was all settled, I decided to take a walk down to the center of the camp. Right near the cafeteria a young man walked up to me. "Aren't you Alcyon Logan?"

I thought he looked familiar, but wasn't sure. "Yes."

"I met you a few years ago at Laurelwood. Our group from Columbia was there to give a program. Eugene Sample introduced us. I guess we are sort of related."

Then I remembered. He was the one whose grandmother married Grandpa Stover. "Now, I remember," I told him. His name was George.

We stood there talking. He asked about my family, about Eugene, and told me something of his family. He told me that he was taking theology at Walla Walla College. Finally, he asked, "Would you like to go to meeting with me tonight?"

I was surprised, but it seemed like it wouldn't be wrong to go to a meeting with someone with a connection to our family. "That would be nice."

"Maybe I should walk to your tent with you, so I'll know where to come." And we walked off together.

I found Enid and told her about my encounter. "I'll meet you after the meeting at the youth tent. I don't know if you have heard of George Chalker. He is coming to take me to the meeting." And I told her about the family connection.

She laughed, "It didn't take you long to find a friend, did it?"

Mrs. Currant and I ate a lunch in our tent. I told her about George, and he came right on time.

The meeting was inspiring, and the music outstanding. I was so thrilled to be at campmeeting with all of these Adventist young people. We met Enid after the meeting, and George and I walked with her to her tent. Walking away, George commented, "She seems like a very nice girl. Did you say that her name is Venden?"

"Yes, I met her when she lived with her Uncle Dan during their campaign in Salem. We've been friends ever since."

"The Venden brothers have been an inspiration to me," George commented. "In fact, since I am interested in music, I would like to be a singing evangelist some day."

Before leaving me at the tent, he asked, "Do you usually go to the early morning meetings at the youth pavilion?"

"I haven't been here before to tent, but I want to go to all the meetings I can."

"I'll come for you if you would like." I saw that George planned to take me to all the meetings. I liked his company, and he seemed like a real Christian gentleman, but I thought, *He's a college man, and I'm only sixteen. He probably thinks I'm older. And I'm afraid Papa would take a pretty dim view of my going around the grounds here with a fellow the minute I arrive. I would be embarrassed to tell him that my father doesn't let me go with boys. If they come on Sabbath, whatever shall I do?*

The truth was that I had never formally had any dates or boy friends, only special friends at the academy. I was quite flattered that a college fellow, taking theology, would be interested in me. *Well, Sabbath was still three days away. I wouldn't worry about it yet.*

The next day George was there to take me to every meeting, and we were getting acquainted. Enid was with us most of the time.

Late Thursday afternoon, George told me, "I have a good friend I want you to meet. We went to Columbia together, and now we are in college. We often sing in the same groups. By the way, someone told me that you play the piano."

We were walking up to the Fleck's tent near the youth pavilion. "It is that one right over there," and he pointed to one on the end of a row, right near the path.

"I see their car is parked by the tent. Kenny lives on a dairy farm, so he has to be home part of the time to help with the milking, but I think he planned to be here tonight."

Coming closer, we saw that someone was sitting at the wheel, lying back, sound asleep. George walked up and tapped him on the arm through the open window.

His friend jerked awake and sat up and smiled. "Oh! Sorry. I was getting a little nap. We got up early this morning to milk."

"That's all right, old pal. I just wanted you to meet a new friend of mine, Alcyon Logan."

By then Ken was fully awake, and we stood by the car visiting with him. Later, when George and I were walking to meeting we went by to get Enid and she sat with us. When the meeting was out we stood talking to friends when Kenny Fleck walked up.

"Well, I'm fully awake now." Then, turning to me, "I'm afraid I didn't make a very good impression today. I was pretty groggy."

George wanted to introduce Enid. "By the way, Kenny, have you met Enid Venden? She's a friend of Alcyon's."

Looking at her intently, Kenny asked, "Did you say, Venden, Enid Venden?"

She smiled and nodded. "Am I supposed to know you?"

"I'm not sure we've met," Ken went on, "but I have heard about you. You see, Melvin and Ivy Venden come to see my folks some times. Ivy and my mom are first cousins. I think she told me about you."

Enid blushed. The truth was that Ivy had told her about Kenny, too. It wasn't hard for them to strike up a friendship. The four of us walked away together. From then on we all sat together at the meetings, and Kenny would walk Enid to her tent.

Later, when she and I were together, I asked her what she thought of Kenneth Fleck. "I don't know him very well yet, but he is really friendly and seems like a good Christian young man. It is true that Aunt Ivy wanted me to meet him. At least it is fun to meet these two nice college fellows. It will make campmeeting more interesting!"

Friday evening, there was a special meeting at the adult auditorium. The four of us sat together in the balcony.

Just as the meeting was closing, Eugene found us. "Alcyon, your folks are here and looking for you."

It was like a bombshell hit me! They weren't supposed to come until the next day. I had planned to tell George that I would be with my parents that day. I turned to him, "Sorry, I'll have to go and find them."

"I'll come with you," he said, getting out of his seat to join me. "I would like to meet them."

I was panic-stricken! We walked down the incline, and I tried several times to tell him I could see him later. I would need to try to find them. But it didn't work. He had no idea of my panic, and I was embarrassed to tell him. Papa would be capable of telling me to pack up and go home with them. But while I was still looking for some way to escape, we ran right into Mama, Papa, Wayne and LaBreta! There was nothing for me to do but introduce my escort.

George, totally unaware of my predicament, put on his very best manners. "I'm so glad to meet you, Mr. and Mrs. Logan. Did you just come?"

Papa was giving him a real once over, and I was holding my breath. Mama understood my dilemma, and tried to keep the conversation light.

But soon, Papa said, "Well, we need to go, Hazel. Let's take Alcyon up to her tent."

I fully expected it to be to pack up my clothes, when George spoke up, "No, you don't need to do that, Mr. Logan. I'll take her. We'll see you to the car first."

I held my breath, but wonder of wonders, Papa said, "All right, the car is down this way."

George never knew how he had so innocently broken the ice for me. Believe it or not, George arranged for my parents to meet his parents. They invited our family to have lunch with them the second Sabbath. And Papa accepted! Years later I asked him about that night.

He said, "Well, I could see he was a clean, decent young man, and you were safe with him."

I guess my poor papa had thought I really needed protecting. From that moment on, he never interfered in my friendships.

Enid told me that she had seen Kenny before and thought he was really great, but had never met him. She had George to thank for that. We had a great time the rest of that week. We attended all the meetings, took walks and got quite well acquainted. When we all left for our homes, it was with an exchange of addresses, but we were still only good friends.

Enid and I did some intense girl talk, discussing these two fellows, wondering if anything would come of it.

Chapter 32

Sabbath At Silver Creek Falls

I called Enid about a possible job for the summer. "The cannery in Silverton is looking for more help. Are you interested?"

"If this is a way to earn some money, yes," she answered.

I called the cannery and got us both on the belt sorting green beans.

She came to my place, and Quentin took us over there to look for a place to live. We found a nice Adventist family, the Emerys, with several small children and a large house. They were willing and eager to rent out the large front bedroom and allow us to use their kitchen. We moved in and went to work. It wasn't easy, bending over that belt eight hours a day, sorting the beans, but we had a great time.

One evening after working all day Mr. Emery called me to the phone. It was George. "Alcyon, do you and Enid have plans for this Sabbath?"

"No, not as far as I know."

"Well, I just talked to Kenny, and we would like to come over this coming Sabbath to spend the day with you two."

Without even asking Enid I answered, "As far as I know it would be great. I'm sure she will agree."

"Good! It might be best if we just meet you at the Silverton church for Sabbath School. You girls just plan the day. Whatever you decide will be fine with us."

As soon as I hung up the phone on the kitchen wall I rushed to our room. "You aren't going to believe this!" I told Enid.

"Whatever happened?" Enid questioned. She could see I was excited.

"George and Kenny are coming to see us this Sabbath! I hope it's OK with you. I was sure it would be! George said they would meet us at the church and would be happy with whatever we planned."

Enid's eyes lit up. She was thrilled, and we made our plans.

We were all on time and sat together. Some one in the audience knew the fellows and knew that they both sang well. They were asked to sing for church. George had a piece of music with him for me at the piano. They had sung that song together many times and knew all the words by memory, "That One Lost Sheep". It was really beautiful. Their tenor voices blended so well, and they sang with pathos. There was a strong chorus of Amens.

My parents had decided that the project at Hubbard was too big for them. They didn't have the needed capital, so they moved back to Salem.

I had called Mom and asked, "Is it all right if Enid and I come for dinner this Sabbath and bring some friends with us? George and Kenny are coming to spend the day with us."

"Of course. We would love having you. Don't worry. I'll have dinner ready."

After church I told the fellows. "Enid and I just have a room in the Emery's house, so I called my Mom, and she is preparing dinner for us."

"That's nice of your folks to invite us," Kenny said. "I don't think I have met them."

Mom had a great dinner, as I knew she would. My father treated them with all courtesy, and he treated me like a young lady that had grown up. After dinner Kenny and George wanted to drive us up to Silver Creek Falls. It was a beautiful summer day.

We took the long walk around the various falls. During the afternoon George and I talked about many things when he made it clear that he wanted to pursue our friendship. At the end of that day at the falls, we drove back to Silverton where Enid and I had prepared a lunch.

When the fellows left that night, Enid and I had a lot to talk about. We were close friends and could share our real feelings. One thing we agreed on, George and Kenny were the caliber of fellows that we wanted for friends.

When the cannery closed at the end of the season, Enid went home, and I went to Salem. I knew that college was out of the question for that year.

My mother had found a young single piano and organ teacher and wanted me to take lessons from him. He was on the eccentric order but a fine musician. He came to our house for the piano lessons, and he helped me rent an organ at a church for my practice and lessons.

There was never any hint of improper conduct on his part, but I soon realized that I might be his favorite pupil. He gave me every consideration. That fall his aunt, who had a lovely place in the country, gave a dinner in his honor, inviting all his students. There would be a recital after the dinner. I was a little surprised that, instead of a solo, he gave me a duet to play with him.

It was to be a formal affair, and Mama helped me to have an appropriate dress. Quentin was invited to come with me, although he wasn't taking lessons. When we went to the candlelit table, there were place cards, and I found that my card was to my teacher's right.

Quentin told me later, "I overheard the aunt talking to another woman who was helping. They are hoping William makes it with you!"

I liked and respected William, but he was definitely not my type, and, besides I was writing to George. Nothing was said to me, and I continued my lessons. I was thrilled to learn to play the organ, and my teacher never once made any inappropriate moves.

When Thanksgiving came around, I had just had my 17 birthday, and George came to visit me for the weekend. The folks thought it would be nice to go out to Falls City for church and have dinner at Grandma's house. Eugene was there, and was glad to see George. He must have arranged for someone to ask George to preach, because he sang and preached that day. On the way home, Quentin was driving with me in the middle and George near the window. The rest of the family was in the back seat.

When George put his arm up around me on the back of the seat, Papa touched his arm, and made some kind of a remark like, "What's that there for?"

Again, innocently, George replied. "Oh, it's more comfortable that way." Papa gave up and didn't say anything more.

That evening George and I went for a ride out to visit a friend. When we came back, sitting in front of our house, we talked. I learned that his interest in me was more than just friendship. I realized then that I wasn't ready to "go steady" with an older fellow, who had more serious intentions than I was ready for. I told him I would rather just be friends. He was hurt, but a gentleman, and so we continued our friendship on a more casual basis. I assured him that he was free to date other girls.

I wasn't sure how things were with Enid and Kenny, but apparently it also stayed on a friendship basis, and they still corresponded occasionally.

Chapter 33

Romance in California

Soon after Christmas, Enid went to the Bay area near San Francisco. She had a friend who was working down there. Housework jobs were plentiful and pay was higher.

She wrote to me, "I have a job here in a wealthy home as a maid. I can earn $50 a month and my room and board. Why don't you come? There are at least 30 girls from the Northwest down here working in affluent homes. We all go to the Burlingame church."

I talked to my parents. Since it was to be with Enid they didn't object. They knew that housemaid jobs in the Salem area paid $15 to $20 a month. When she wrote again, saying there was a job open for me, I decided to go. It was quite a venture, taking the bus by myself to San Mateo, and I was glad that Enid was there to meet me.

Our places of employment were within walking distance, and we spent all of our free time together. We were disappointed to find that many of the girls went to restaurants and even theaters on Sabbath.

"Let's take sack lunches," Enid suggested. "And we can take the street car to parks and even to Golden Gate Park in San Francisco to spend the Sabbath."

And that is what we did. We were both able to have Sabbaths free and work on Sundays. I had learned how to cook, keep house and take care of children at home with my mother. But this was a new experience.

The woman where I worked was a socialite. The house was a mansion. The week's work was all scheduled out on a list, and divided in such a way that none of the days were hard. I learned to cook for formal dinners, and to do everything in a way that was very proper. The lady of the house was cultured, though not a professing Christian. She didn't smoke, but her husband did, and they drank wine on special occasions.

One day I was alone in the house, cleaning the front rooms. On the beautiful coffee table was a fancy china box. While I was dusting I discovered it contained cigarettes, but not ordinary ones. The aroma was tempting. I had never smoked a cigarette or tasted alcohol. A strong temptation hit me. I wondered what it would be like to just try one. No one would ever know.

Suddenly, I closed the lid! *Whatever was I thinking! I have never touched tobacco or strong drink.* I was never tempted with cigarettes again.

But another temptation awaited. There had been a formal dinner, and I had served wine at the end. It wasn't ordinary wine, but very expensive. After filling the goblets, there was just a little left in the bottle. *It smells good. What does it taste like? One little taste wouldn't hurt.* Again, I pushed the bottle away! *I will never touch it!*

One of my friends from Laurelwood worked in San Francisco in an office and lived with some teachers. Yvonne called one day, "The teachers, who live with me are gone for the weekend. I've invited a friend for dinner and he is bringing his friend, Bob. Would you like to join us?"

Bob was a tall, blonde, Danish young man, who had been raised Lutheran. He was clean cut, didn't drink or smoke and had a good job in carpentry and studied evenings to be an architect.

There was a piano in the house, and after the dinner, Yvonne asked me to play. She loved to sing, and wanted me to play some of our favorite hymns. We spent the rest of the afternoon that way. Bob sat there enjoying the music.

Later Yvonne and her friend were in the other room talking, and that left us alone. Bob wanted to know all about me, and told me about himself. His mother had died, and his father was alone. He was very close to his family.

When I had to take the train back to San Mateo, Bob took me to the station. Before I boarded the train, he said, "Alcyon, it's been fun to know you. Can I call you?"

He called that week, and we arranged to meet the next Sabbath. I told him it would have to be after church. He wanted to take me to the center of town to see some special decorations since he was also an artist.

I explained, "I would rather not go to town until after sundown," and then told him about my Sabbath.

"I respect you for that," he said. "I'll never ask you to do it again." We went to an art museum and he pointed out all the famous artists and their paintings. I could see he had been there many times.

He asked me to go to the theater. I just smiled at him, "No, I don't go to shows." This was all new for him, but he seemed sincerely interested. Later he told me, "I've never known a girl like you before. They are hard to find."

We continued to meet on weekends, and he always took me to a place that was appropriate for Sabbath. He brought his camera one day and told me that he wanted to take my picture to send to his father and sister. I learned that he was also an amateur photographer. He took all kinds of poses, and gave me copies.

I soon realized that Bob was not thinking of me as just another girl. He told me, "I have always wanted to know a girl like you."

I knew that I would never marry someone not of my faith, but I was sure he would be willing to learn. I was of an artistic bent and appreciated his love for the arts and finer things. He dressed in the best taste, and took me to the nicest restaurants. There were things about him that were very appealing, but I knew I wasn't ready for a serious relationship, and especially with one not of my faith. And, after all, I wanted to be a missionary. He didn't fit into that picture, but still I enjoyed his company.

It was the Christmas season. One day I was shopping in town, when, suddenly, I had a tremendous urge to go home for Christmas. Homesickness had never been a problem for me, but the desire was so strong, my eyes filled with tears. But I knew I couldn't take off from my work.

I had taken over a job where another Adventist girl had been working for several years. Her mother became seriously ill and needed for her to come home. I agreed to work in her place. If she were able to come back later, I would find another job, and if she didn't, the job would be mine.

When I learned that Mary wanted her job back, it was just the answer I needed. I would go home for Christmas! I would find another job when I came back.

When I told Bob about my plans he was devastated. "But I already have tickets for us to go and hear Jeanette McDonald and Nelson Eddy at the Opera House! Can't you wait and go a little later?"

"I'm sorry, but my plans are made. You can write and tell me about the concert."

Although I had no other plan than to return in a few weeks, Bob was afraid I wouldn't come and was constantly trying to make me promise that I would. "My sister lives in Tacoma. Maybe I can come and see you and visit her, too."

"That would be great," I replied.

The day I was to leave, he took me to the Greyhound bus depot. We stood there talking, waiting for me to board. He was still asking, "When will you be back?"

"I don't know yet, but I'll let you know," I promised.

The driver of the bus went up to the door, ready to take the tickets. Bob took me in his arms and asked, "Alcyon, can I kiss you goodbye?"

I looked straight into his eyes and answered, "No, Bob, I made a vow some time ago that the next man who kisses me will be the one I marry."

"Then, I will kiss you in 1940." That was the end of 1939, and Bob stood there waving until we were out of sight.

That long trip home gave me lots of time to think and ponder my future. While I liked and admired Bob, I knew I was not in love with him. I was just 18, and still had illusions of a college education.

But, I also knew that I would probably still date him when I went back. He was a safe person to be with in that big city environment. He knew all the nice places to go, and he respected my religion. I wondered why I had never made an effort to take him to church with me. He knew my standards, but he really didn't know much about my faith. *There will be time for that when I go back,* I decided.

Chapter 34

Just Friends?

It was wonderful to be home. I had spent almost the rest of my month's wages to buy presents for all the family. My little sister, LaBreta, was my special pet and I brought her a beautiful big doll. We were all home together. By then Quentin and I had yielded to the customs of the day, and called our parents, Mom and Pop. Our father thought that Dad was disrespectful. There was seven year old LaBreta, Wayne, almost twelve, and Quentin, twenty. I loved being in the kitchen again with Mom.

Soon after arriving, a card came from Bob. It was a watercolor he had painted himself. Enclosed there was a letter. "I miss you so much. I went to the Opera and since I already had your ticket, there was an empty seat beside me. When are you coming back? I took pictures at the concert."

I hadn't told my parents about him. Now, it was time to do that. "Bob is just a good friend. It's really nice to have a trustworthy escort in the San Francisco area!" I joked.

Mom wanted to know all about him. My father didn't say much.

I wrote to Bob and told him about my trip, about my family and our Christmas.

The next letter included the program from the Nelson Eddy concert, as well as pictures Bob had taken. "It was lonesome sitting there by myself."

One day I was reading in *Steps to Christ*. I had been thinking a lot about my future. What should be my next step? Should I go back to California? I had a strong sense that I was at a crossroad in my life. Little did I realize of the critical difference my choice would make in my future.

After reading in my book and in the Bible, I knelt by my bed. "Lord, I need your direction. You know all about me. Help me to make right choices. Most of all, help me to know the plan you have for my life."

After Christmas and New Years, Quentin and I decided to go to Walla Walla for a weekend. We had two cousins there, Eugene Sample, and Esther Logan. Enid had decided to come home for a vacation too. We arranged to pick her up at her home in White Salmon. We drove through a snowstorm all the way through the Columbia Gorge, on the old highway.

I stayed with Esther in Conard Hall and Quentin stayed with Eugene. He must have told George that we were coming, because his parents, who had moved close to the college, had prepared a dinner for all of us on Sabbath. George and I had written once in a while, as we had remained friends. He asked me to go with him to the Saturday evening program at the college, and Enid had a date with a friend of some old friends. I kidded her, "so you have a blind date?"

When we arrived back home, my father told me, "That Fleck fella' was here for church on Sabbath and he was looking for you."

"Oh, really? What was he doing here?"

"He is helping Elder Patterson with an evangelistic effort in McMinnville. He is in charge of the music. I could tell that he is interested in you."

"Don't be silly!" I laughed. "He likes Enid, not me. They have drifted apart, but I'm sure he'll want to see her again." Then thinking about it, I continued, "You know, why don't we go over to their meetings next Sunday night. I'll get Enid to come and spend the next weekend with me, and invite him to come over, too. I think that distance has pulled them apart."

We made plans to all go to the meeting on Sunday night. That morning, a friend of my parents called, "My wife is sick. Do you know of someone I can get to come and stay with her?"

My father asked me if I would like to go. I consented, and the man was grateful. I spent most of that day at Mrs. Bell's house, but planned to leave in time to get ready to go to McMinnville. In the afternoon, the phone rang, and it was for me.

"Alcyon, this is Kenny."

"Do you mean, Kenny Fleck?" I was surprised. "Where are you calling from?"

"Actually, I'm right here in Salem, but have to leave to get back for meeting tonight. I was glad to hear you are home."

"It's great to hear you, Kenny. It's strange. We were going to come to your meeting tonight."

"That's wonderful. Please be sure and come!"

After catching up a little more on what had been going on in our lives, we hung up, but not before he told me again, "Be sure to come. I'll be watching for you."

There was nothing in the conversation to indicate anything more than our old friendship in our foursome. Ken and I had always joked back and forth a lot. We were more outgoing than either Enid or George.

The meetings were held in a tabernacle erected for that purpose. The song service was in progress as we came in and found a seat about half way up on the left side. Ken was directing the music.

There was a flash of a smile as he saw us come in. There was something else. Some people call it electricity. When the preaching started he sat in the front seat on the right side near the piano. For some reason, every time I looked his direction, he was looking my way, and then we would both look the other direction. I have to confess, I didn't get much out of the sermon that night.

My father had told me that Kenny was interested in me, but I knew that wasn't true. It couldn't be. Besides Enid was my friend. But something definitely was different. When the meeting was over, Ken was back at the door with Pastor Patterson, shaking hands and greeting the people. I still wanted to invite him to come over and see Enid. We waited until he was free to talk.

I was stunned when he grabbed my hand and, looking right into my eyes, said, "I don't know who I would rather see come in that door than you, Alcyon."

But I was not going to believe that he meant anything special toward me. After all, I knew he was a very friendly person. Then I told him that Enid was in Portland, and I hoped she was coming to visit me the next Sabbath. "Could you come, too?"

"Well, I don't know if I can. My time is pretty well programmed here with the meetings. I would like to come, but I am sure Enid has other plans. We haven't been in touch for months."

In the corner of the back seat on the way home, I was very quiet. I couldn't figure out what was happening. Kenny Fleck was a theology student from Walla Walla. He was the singing evangelist in Elder Patterson's meetings. I was an eighteen year old, who had not yet entered college. *I must have mistaken the signals I felt from him. I must not let myself believe he is interested in me.*

Chapter 35

Could It Be True?

"Alcyon, Kenny Fleck is looking for you," Wayne told me as I walked in the door to a district youth meeting at the church.

Enid couldn't come for the weekend, and I hadn't heard from Ken. A friend in Salem, Mary Oliver, had invited me home for Sabbath dinner.

Soon, Ken appeared, apparently waiting for me. "Good to see you, Alcyon. They have asked me to sing for this meeting. Would you play for me?"

"I'd be glad to. What are you going to sing?"

"I have the music here, 'Hold Thou My Hand.' Maybe we should go down to one of the children's rooms and run over it."

I led the way, knowing my way around the church. We went through the song a couple times before going upstairs to find a seat near the piano. It was obvious to me that things were not the same. If he wasn't trying to work something up with me, he was certainly letting it look that way.

Mom and Pop Logan were sitting a few seats behind us, and I learned later that they were more than pleased to see this promising young man with their daughter. Maybe it was partly because of their concern over my relationship with Bob, whom they didn't know.

At the end of the meeting, Ken asked if he could take me home.

"I came with Mary. I suppose I should stay with her."

Ken took that as a reject and walked away. I saw him go to his old Durant, and peel around the corner. I really meant to infer that he should invite Mary to come with us. *I guess I blew it this time. This is probably the end of any interest he might have had in me,* I thought with dismay.

The next day the phone rang. "Alcyon, this is Kenny. I'm in town with the Pattersons. I wonder if I could come over."

"Of course. I'll be happy to have you."

Then he added, "Did Enid come?"

"No, I'm sorry she couldn't make it." I was so afraid of mistaking his attentions to me, I thought he was disappointed.

But in a few minutes the doorbell rang, and there stood Kenny with a big bouquet of flowers. I could see the Pattersons out in the car. They were having a lot of fun at his expense, knowing what I didn't know, that he wouldn't have taken the flowers in if Enid were there.

He stayed several hours. We renewed our friendship and more. Ken always had a way with people, and he won my father over right from the start. Pop wanted some music, so we went to the piano, and I played while Ken sang. His beautiful, clear tenor voice thrilled my music loving father, as well as my mother.

"Could we go for a walk?" he suggested.

"Would you like to walk up to the Capitol grounds?" We lived just a few blocks away.

"I'd like that. Let's go."

A beautiful park surrounds the Oregon State Capitol. We walked through the paths, talking and getting acquainted on a different level.

He asked me, "I've heard that your little sister and brother sing together. Could you bring them over to the meetings and give us special music?"

"I'm sure we can arrange it. When would you like us to come?"

"How about this week, maybe Wednesday night?"

"We can talk to the folks when we go back to the house."

As we walked toward home, Ken told me, "I would love to take you to Longview to meet my parents. Would you be willing to go?"

"I would like that," I smiled at him.

The Pattersons would be coming for him, so we hurried back home. When he asked my father about coming over and bringing Wayne and LaBreta to sing, Pop was happy to arrange it. Before leaving Ken took my hand. "I'll be looking forward to seeing you Wednesday night."

After he left, I went to the kitchen to find my mom. She smiled at me. "Well, Alcyon, what is going on with you and Kenneth Fleck?"

We sat down at the kitchen table. "I don't know, Mom. I don't know what to think. Do you think he could be serious about me?"

"Well, I guess time will tell. In the meantime, just hang on to your heart!"

When I walked into the tabernacle on Wednesday evening, my heart was pounding. When he called on us for the special music, Wayne and LaBreta walked up and I went to the piano. They always did a beautiful job. Wayne sang the melody and she sang alto.

After the meeting, the Pattersons told us, "You must come back and bring the children to sing again."

Ken thanked us profusely and began to arrange another time when they could sing. I remembered that his birthday was in March. "Don't you have a birthday coming up?"

Surprised, he answered, "Well, actually I guess I do. It's next Monday."

"How about coming to our house to celebrate?" I suggested.

"I would love that," he smiled. "But don't worry about doing anything special."

Mom and I planned a special birthday dinner and the day went great. Ken has always been very appreciative, especially of good food. He praised Mom's cooking profusely.

"Well, Alcyon and I did it together," she told him. Again, we entertained my father with some music. Pop would sit and listen to music just as long as we kept on playing and singing. I discovered that I loved to accompany Ken. We seemed to really be in sync.

That next Sunday night Wayne and LaBreta sang for the meeting again. When Ken and I talked at the close, he asked me, "Could we just take a little walk down to the corner?"

As we walked away from the crowd he wanted to know, "What is your status with George now?"

"We are good friends, but we haven't been going together for a long time. What about you and Enid?'

"I respect and admire her a lot, but we were never anything but friends. I haven't heard from her in months."

As we walked back, he urged me to come again on Wednesday night. "You know, with meetings in the evenings, and helping Glenn with the visiting, it is hard for me to get away, but I do want to see you."

"I don't know. I can't promise this week."

When Wednesday came, I asked Quentin if he would take me over to McMinnville that evening.

"Why don't you let him come here? Don't chase him! Besides, there isn't enough gas."

That discouraged me, and I certainly didn't want to chase him, so I gave up the idea.

But later that afternoon I had such an urge to go to McMinnville I couldn't seem to resist it. I went to my mother, "Mom, you know Kenny asked me to come for meeting tonight, but Quentin won't take me."

"Why not?" she asked.

"He doesn't think I should go, and he says there isn't enough gas in the car."

"Don't worry, I'll give you money for gas." My mom was always on my side.

When I told Quentin, he warned me about chasing the guy, but agreed to go. By the time we arrived, I almost had cold feet. What if it was a mistake for me to come? But it was too late to back out now. We walked in.

Ken was in front, leading the music. Claris Patterson was at the piano. It was situated so she faced the platform. Later, she told me, "I could tell when you walked in, just watching Kenny's face! It really lit up."

Ken had also been looking for guidance from God. For some reason, maybe because of my fear of trusting that he was serious, he had felt insecure in whether or not I would accept him. He had called his mother and told her, "I think I've found the girl I want to marry if I can get her."

That day he felt impressed to pray, "If this is your will, if Alcyon is the one for me, please bring her to meeting tonight."

Later, retelling the story, he laughed, "No wonder my face lit up!"

That incident was significant. In comparing notes later, we were both convinced that God was interested in us and our prayers were being answered.

Our family went the last Sunday night of the meetings. As we walked out, Elder Patterson asked me to wait until he finished greeting the people, he wanted to talk to me. I wondered what on earth he would want to say to me. Maybe he didn't approve!

When he stepped over to where I was waiting he said, "You know, Alcyon, our team here, my family, our Bible worker, Mrs. Detamore and Kenny, are going to the beach tomorrow afternoon, and coming back the next day. I know that Kenny would have a better time if you were along. How about it? You could stay at our house tonight."

"I don't know. I'll have to talk to my mom."

When I told my mother, she thought I should go.

"But I don't have any extra clothes here," I worried.

"Well, let's see." Mom was trying to think of a way. "Why don't I put some things on the bus for you. They will come in the morning."

It was arranged. Ken took me to the Pattersons in his old Durant. On the way it was his bad luck to be spotted by a patrolman. *What luck!* he thought to himself. *The first time I get her in my car, and this has to happen.*

The old Durant had many defects, but the patrolman was interested in the lack of a taillight. "I'll get it fixed right away," Ken promised, and the officer let us go. His embarrassment was relieved when I thought it was funny!

My package did come the next morning. Claris Patterson prepared the food basket and packed their clothes. By the time we were in the car, ready to go, it was past noon.

We went by the Bacchus' home where Ken was staying. He opened an upstairs window. "I'll be right there. Mrs. Bacchus is ironing my pants!"

"Well, you'd better wait!" Glenn replied, and everyone in the car had a good laugh. When Ken finally emerged, properly dressed, we were on our way.

The Pattersons and their two small children, Jeannie and Gary, sat in front. Mrs. Detamore sat with us in the back, with me in the middle. It was cold on the way. The heater didn't seem to be working right so we put a blanket over our laps, which made it great for handholding.

When we arrived in Tillamook, Glenn suggested, "It's getting late. Do you folks think we should find a motel here?"

There was a full moon that night, and we had been looking forward to a walk on the beach. Ken reached across and whispered to Mrs. Detamore, "Please tell them you would rather go on to the coast."

"You know," she spoke up, "I think it would be nicer to go on and find a place at the beach, where we can sleep listening to the ocean!"

We could have hugged her when Glenn agreed, and started on down the road toward Rockaway.

Chapter 36

Moonlight on the Sand

They found a two-bedroom cabin right on the beach. While the Pattersons were arranging things for the night and getting their sleepy children tucked in, Mrs. Detamore put a motherly hand on Ken's shoulder and said, "Why don't you two run along now and have your stroll?"

We didn't need any more encouragement. Soon we were down on the sand. I broke the silence, "What a beautiful sight!"

The moon shimmered across the breakers as they rolled in, making a path toward us. We stood, looking far out over the endless sea, letting the beauty of the moment wash over us.

"There is something special about the ocean for me," Ken commented. "When I need inspiration there is no better place for me to come. I am always overwhelmed with the realization of the mighty power of God. He bids the waves to come here, but no farther."

The wind was brisk, and I drew the coat Claris had loaned closer around me. "We'd better walk, we'll keep warmer," Ken suggested.

As we strolled down the beach, we talked of many things, especially updating events in our lives since we had been a foursome at Silver Creek Falls. Then the conversation took a more serious turn.

"Are you still planning to finish your ministerial course, Kenny?"

"Oh yes, my parents dedicated me to the Lord's work when I was born. Somehow, I can never escape the idea that God has called me to preach. I am planning to go back and finish as soon as circumstances permit. The opportunity came to help in this evangelistic campaign, and I felt it would be good experience since my funds were too low for college this quarter anyway."

Then he asked, "What are your plans for the future, Alcyon?"

"Well, of course my first goal is to finish my education. Since I was a child, I always dreamed of being a missionary, a missionary in Africa. The last few months have been a time of indecision for me, but I still want to be in God's work in some way. My folks would like for me to go on with music. I'm just not sure what I will do."

"By the way, Alcyon, I don't mind telling you that you are my favorite accompanist at the moment. I liked the way you did the song I sang at the Salem church. I think you should keep up with your music, if you want my advice."

"Thanks, Kenny. You are my favorite tenor too!"

We were coming to the last of the beach houses. Looking back, I commented, "It looks like we have come a long way! The lights look pretty small from where we started."

"Yes, I guess you are right. All good things have to come to an end. This is one of those times I would like for time to stand still."

Heading back, we walked along in silence a little while, and then Ken spoke. "Alcyon, would you mind my asking you a question?" He hesitated, feeling a bit awkward. "I have been wondering if there is someone else, any other young man, that matters to you?"

I didn't answer immediately. I hesitated to tell him about Bob, but I knew I must be honest with him. Finally, in a quiet voice, I began, "In a way there has been someone. I write to a guy in San Francisco. There is no commitment between us. How about you? I wouldn't have mentioned it if you hadn't brought it up, but I heard that you have a girl friend at Walla Walla."

He admitted that it was true but hastily added, "Until you came along, Alcyon, I was still scouting. But, as of today, no one interests me but you. How would you feel about writing that fellow in California? Tell him that you don't have time to write him any more?" Ken was smiling.

"Yes, I would be willing to write that to him," I answered simply.

"I guess I had better write a letter too. I'll get it off soon."

As we neared the lights of our cabin, Ken picked up a stick, and began writing in the sand. He drew a very large heart. I watched as he drew the thrilling words, I LOVE YOU, in the middle of the heart.

I looked long at the words in the sand and then looked up to him. My lips said nothing, but he saw the smile in my eyes.

We walked on toward the cabin, his arm around me, holding me close. It was a precious moment in time. To this day Ken always draws the big heart and those special words in the sand every time that we go to the beach.

Chapter 37

In Love

The rest of our group in the cabin didn't know about the heart in the sand, but they must have seen the glow on our faces.

The next morning we went down to the beach one more time. Ken told me about the letter he would need to write. "She is a nice girl, but she just doesn't have what I want."

When I asked him about a girl that I knew held a candle for him, he replied, "You know, I have had several girl friends that I admire and respect a lot. But, I have always wanted a wife that would make my blood tingle, and none of them ever affected me that way!"

I wondered what category I would fall in!

When he put me on a bus for Salem, I went with stars in my eyes, and my heart in the clouds. All the way home, the refrain was running through my mind, "I am in love!" Although I had not told him, I knew that I was really in love. Of all the friends I had had, contrary to some girls, I knew that I had not fallen for any of them. *I am in love! I am really in love! Oh, I hope this is the real thing for Kenny, too.*

A few days later, one of our neighbors, an elderly woman, who needed someone to stay with her at nights, called. Mom asked me if I wanted the job. I knew I could use a little extra money, so agreed to go. Just before leaving my father told me, "By the way, Kenny called. He was leaving for Longview, and said to tell you goodbye."

I was devastated. I knew he was leaving for home soon, but was sure he wouldn't go without coming to see me first. But to just leave like that with a casual message! My old fears rose to the surface. Could it be possible that I had been an utter fool, that he didn't mean anything after all? I cried in my pillow half the night. How could I have been taken in like that? The problem was that he had really captured my heart. I had never let that happen before.

When I went back home in the morning, I wasn't talking much. But when Pop came into the kitchen he said, "Oh, I forgot to tell you that Kenny said he would be back this week and would call you."

I nearly collapsed, but didn't want anyone to know what I had gone through. My father never realized what a cruel joke he had played on me.

Ken did call, and I knew that he was indeed serious about loving me. He said, "I'm going to be packing up my things and driving home this next weekend. Would you go with me? I so much want my parents to meet you."

Without acting too eager, I was happy to accept the invitation. Driving a hundred miles in the old Durant was as thrilling as if it had been a limousine. We visited and became more acquainted as we rode along. In fact one of the things that made me very sure that Kenny Fleck was my ideal of a man was that we enjoyed each other's company so much. We could discuss any topic with enthusiasm, whether it was politics, psychological theories, or spiritual themes.

When we turned into the lane that led to their farm, I saw the house in the distance. Soon, I saw a black dog racing toward us. "Oh, that is Ring! He knows my car and he knows me!"

It was evening when we arrived. The early spring day was cool, and there was a fire in their wood heater. Ken brought me in, and we stood in the middle of the room. His mother had greeted us at the door. It seemed like the room was full of people, just looking me over. There were his parents.

Then there was his Grandma Lashier; he had told me a lot about her. A tall, slim older lady stood in the back of the room, that was Aunt Alice, his father's maiden sister. A middle-aged man sat quietly in a rocker near the stove. "This is Uncle Harold," Ken told me. I learned that he was Grandma Lashier's only son and youngest child. "He is a doctor, on a visit here." There was one person missing, his sister, Jean, at college.

I could sense that it was quite an event for Ken to bring a girl home. However, I was not aware that he had already announced that I was the girl he hoped to marry. It was an experience that we often rehearsed in years to come, the once-over that I endured at my initiation into his family. I still had not understood how close this family was, and the place Ken had as the first child and first grandchild. It was no wonder that it mattered to them what kind of a girl he brought home!

The next morning he showed me all around the place, and took me to the barn with him when he milked. It was fun to watch the barn cats stand there with their mouths open while he squirted milk into their faces as they tried to capture it with their paws.

When he finished milking he asked me, "Would you like to meet my pony, Billy?"

"Of course. I remember your telling me about that special pony?"

"OK, then, just wait here, and I'll bring him." Soon Ken came riding up on a dappled-gray horse and stopped right near where I was standing.

He proceeded to stand up on the pony's bare back, and then stood on his head. Billy didn't move a muscle, until he got back down and told him, "OK, Billy. You can move now."

When he returned Billy to his pasture, we went in to breakfast.

I learned very quickly that this was a home where the table was loaded with delicious food at mealtime. There was always whole milk on the table, light cream and heavy cream. It was a little intimidating to realize that all the women in that family were known as top notch cooks. I was thankful that, at least, I wasn't ignorant about cooking or housekeeping.

At church on Sabbath I met lots of new people. It was evident that Ken's father was like a patriarch in that church and his mother the church hostess. I was on the spot. Ken was asked to sing, and seemed secretly happy that he could show me off as his accompanist.

Back at home; after the weekend was over, I filled my parents in on all the details. Mom knew about the heart in the sand, and she was happy for me.

There was a letter awaiting me on the dresser in my room. It was from Bob. He sent some more pictures, telling me how much he was missing me, and wanting me to hurry back. There was even a picture he had taken of me. On the back was a caption, "Girl of my Dreams."

I hadn't written the fateful letter yet, sort of dreading it. I knew he would be hurt. I thought long and hard about how to put that kind of news in a letter as gently as possible.

At first I just told him I had met someone that I was interested in, and that he shouldn't wait around for me. Right away a letter came back, begging me to reconsider. He even said, "Even if you have to go with that guy, please still write to me."

Finally, when I knew that my new love was for real, I had to fulfill my promise to Ken, and tell Bob that it was over. I knew then that I had valued him as a friend, but my heart had still not been involved.

I thought back to the days when I first came home, the confusion I felt, the need I knew that I had for God's special guidance in my life. *Could this really be the answer to my prayer? Could Kenny be the one that God has chosen for me? Only time will tell, but I am ready now to really trust God with my life.*

Chapter 38

Will You Be Mine?

Ken found a job working as a driver for an Adventist bakery in Longview. I found odd jobs near our home in Salem. He visited me on some weekends, and on others he paid for me to come to Longview on the bus. I was learning to know his family better, and we were learning to know each other better. We spent hours talking over our concepts about life.

One day, while he was in Salem, we went for a drive and found a quiet place to stop. On that occasion we each shared about our own spiritual journey.

He told about his boyhood on The Lone Juniper Farm, about their home Sabbath Schools. "I will never forget my parents' faithfulness in giving us a real Christian home, where God was the center. But, as I grew up, especially in college, I began to wonder why I am an Adventist. Is it because I was raised that way? I learned that I couldn't just go on what my parents believed or taught. I had to experience it myself."

I listened carefully as he went on. "There was a time when I even questioned the existence of God! I never told Mom and Dad about it. But I began to spend time, thinking these things over, studying and searching for answers. I love nature, the mountains, lakes and woods. Out there, I could look up in the sky at night and realize that there had to be a Creator. Then I knew, that if that was so, the Bible had to be true. And if that was true, then the Adventist Church is the true church. Did you go through that?"

I thought a moment. "I have to say that I never questioned God or my Adventist faith. I did have a problem with the Spirit of Prophecy. You see, my father became an Adventist when he was a young man, then went to Battle Creek to study to be a nurse. While there he heard Mrs. White speak, and was completely convinced that she was sent from God to our church. When I was growing up, he always wanted me to read The Testimonies, and he often called things to my attention, using those books as his reference. I remember asking him to buy a special book for Adventist youth. He answered, 'You have the *Testimonies*. That's enough.'

"I guess when I came to the questioning, rebellious age, I didn't want to hear about the Testimonies any more. But when I began to read them for myself, I found out what a blessing they are, especially to help me understand the Bible better."

"That's interesting," Ken remarked. "You know, one day, when I was sick, I read *Messages to Young People* in one reading. It was a revelation to me. I especially love the little book, *Steps to Christ*."

"I have learned to appreciate those two books, too. At one time, when Enid and I were working in Silverton, we would go up on a nearby bluff and read out of *Steps to Christ* for our morning devotions."

"It is interesting," Ken added. "We have similar backgrounds, long time Adventist families. My father was the youngest of a large family, and he remembers hearing about when an Adventist minister came to their house and stood in front of the fireplace, giving them the message of Jesus' soon coming. That is when his parents were baptized."

Then I told him about my Great-grandpa Stover, who was a pioneer Adventist minister, and my mother's father, who was a minister. "We really have heritages to be thankful for."

We discussed what we believed to be the proper roles for the husband and wife in the family. It wasn't a common subject in those days, but I had my ideas.

"I know that the Bible says that the husband should be the head of the house. I believe that, as long as the husband understands how to treat his wife. I have seen families where the man flaunted that role to gain control, and then abused it. I can see where there needs to be an authority figure in some ways. But Mrs. White does explain that every woman is an individual, accountable to God for herself. I guess my problem is with men who lord it over their wives, not considering their wishes or feelings."

"I agree with that. It seems to me that if people love God and each other, they should be able to live happily in peace."

We had long discussions on many subjects, and seemed to agree on what we wanted in a marriage.

One weekend, when I was in Longview, Ken's mother suggested that I make a pie, a lemon pie. I hadn't done any cooking there, only helped in the kitchen. I looked at Ken, "Is this a test?"

He laughed, but I understood that she wanted to be sure that he was thinking of practical things, and should be sure I knew how to cook.

I accepted the invitation. "Sure, I'll make a lemon pie. Just tell me where the ingredients are."

I had heard that Grandma Lashier was famous for lemon pies, and she was visiting at the time. Maybe it was her idea! They didn't know that lemon pie was one of my specialties. I had made them in the mansion where I worked, and I had made them at home. Actually, it was one of my mom's specialties too. When it came time for dessert, I brought out the pie. I think they all agreed that I had passed the test. Ken even assured me, "It was as good as Grandma's."

Each time we were together our conversations became more personal. We discussed, at great length, our goals for life. Once, Ken specifically asked, "What do you expect of marriage?"

We both shared what we admired in our parents and what we would do differently. I remember asking him what his view was on the roles of husbands and wives in a marriage. In one of these conversations Ken told me, "I'm amazed at the similarity of our backgrounds, and especially of our ideas."

That Sabbath afternoon, Ken took me for a ride up a hill, where you could see over the whole town. We sat up there a long time, our conversation becoming more and more serious. I asked him, "Did your mother have a special reason in asking me to make a pie?"

He laughed. "I suppose she did. She knows how I feel about you. In fact, while I was still in McMinnville I told her, 'I think I've found the girl I want to marry, if I can get her.'"

He looked at me to study my reaction. I just said, "Really?"

On the way home he reminded me, "You've said that you vowed that the next man who kissed you would be the one you marry. Do you think it would be reasonable to kiss someone that you would be willing to marry, even if you aren't engaged yet?"

I thought a moment and then looked at him, smiling. "I guess that would take some thought, wouldn't it?"

By the time we came home it was late. The house was dark, and obviously everyone was asleep. Ring met us out by the gate where we stopped to talk under some huge trees. There was a full moon shining through the trees. Ken had something on his mind, and stopped just inside the gate, taking me into his arms. Ring finally lay down by our feet. The setting could not have been more romantic, when he asked the question, "Will you be mine forever?"

I wasn't really surprised, but had a strange reaction. I literally trembled from head to foot. I didn't have words at that moment, but looked into his face, and just nodded.

When Ken kissed me, Ring looked up at the full moon and began to howl! He kept howling until Ken was afraid he would wake everyone up. He had never done that before and never again to our knowledge. It seems that Ring sensed that something very special had happened that night.

Years later, I wrote a poem and set it to music. The first verse is:

I'm thinking today of that night long ago,
When my heart was first given to you.
You were the fulfillment of my fondest dreams,
And I hoped that you loved me too.
With the full spring moon shining through the tall
  trees,
It was a magical moment in time.
While with strong arms you held me,
You whispered the words,
"Will you forever, my dearest, be mine?"

Chorus:

Darling, just be mine forever.
I can love no one but you.

Our future we'll plan as we go hand in hand.
My heart is for no one but you.

Chapter 39

College With a Struggle

That summer I went canvassing with books from the Oregon Conference. They sent me to Astoria, Oregon. I lived in an Adventist home, and worked all over that town that is literally built on a hill. Ken was working in Longview, and we got together sometimes on the weekends.

At that time, Astoria seemed to be largely Scandinavian people. They were not easy to sell books to, but I did find them to comply when they ordered books. That made deliveries easier. I found people who were anxious to talk about God.

I remember one lady, a single mother of a large family. When she knew I was selling religious books, she invited me in, opening up her heart to me. She couldn't afford a book, but I tried to lead her to Jesus, who could help her with her problems. I had prayer with her and left, feeling that I had brought hope to someone that day.

There were many interesting experiences, but one stood out. One of the books in the series that I was selling was a health book. I had walked up a hill, and then a long flight of stairs. The lady of the house wasn't interested, but she was sure that a friend of hers would be and insisted that I visit her. She was a nurse at the Catholic hospital, and lived in an apartment there. That evening I went to find her.

When she opened the door, and realized what I was doing, she almost began to cry. "You are an Adventist, aren't you? It seems that God finds me wherever I am."

Then she told me about other contacts she had had with Adventists, and how now she was convinced that God had brought me to her. She ordered the books. Then she asked, "Could I go to church with you?"

The next Sabbath I went by for her. A young couple in the church by the name of Rood promised to visit her and give her Bible studies.

When I left for college at the end of the summer I prayed that at least one soul would be saved because of my summer there in Astoria. Several years later, at the Oregon campmeeting in Gladstone, my nurse friend came up to me. "I just want to tell you that God brought you to me that day. I was baptized and have been serving God ever since."

I knew then that, even though I didn't make much money that summer, my time had been well spent. When I went to college that fall my funds were just enough to get registered. But Dean Dorothy Foreman helped me find a home where I could work for my room and board. The place she found was in Walla Walla, and I would need to take the bus back and forth.

"But I don't have money for that," I told her.

She went for her purse and pulled out five dollars. "Here, Alcyon, this will help you get started."

I thanked her profusely. But before moving to that home, Miss Foreman called for me. "I think I have found a better place for you, Alcyon. It is within walking distance, down on Wallulla Road."

She knew that I had been given work at the music conservatory to pay for part of my tuition. "They have two young boys taking piano lessons and want a music student who can tutor them."

I think that Victor Johnson, the violin teacher had recommended me. I worked for him, accompanying violin lessons, tutoring beginning violin students, and playing for the grade school orchestra. I also played violin in the college orchestra. I was thankful I could return the five dollars to Dean Foreman.

My program was more than full, going to school in the mornings, working in the conservatory part of the afternoons, and working my four hours in the home for my room and board. My only time for study was evenings, and I often studied until the wee hours.

Ken started out the quarter, but because of some financial and other reasons, he left to look for work. Although we didn't have much time to be together there, I missed him dreadfully. He had relatives in Los Angeles, where he had prospects of a job.

By the end of the quarter, after studying into the early morning hours for final exams, I realized I was burning the candle at both ends. I missed Ken, and he was hoping I would come and find work near him. By that time, we were both interested in trying to get funds together so we could get married. Then we would go back to college, so I didn't go back that quarter.

The first job Ken found was at the Los Angeles County Hospital. He had never been an orderly, but at that time he was ready for any kind of work. He had only been there a few days, emptying bedpans and cleaning up people in the men's ward, when his name came over the loud speaker. "Mr. Fleck, you are wanted in the morgue."

He didn't know where that was, but found out. When he arrived he was shown a body of a large woman on the table, in the same condition as when she was born. She had just had an autopsy and had an incision the length of her abdomen.

The supervisor told him, "You need to sew her up," then gave him gloves and showed him the thread and needle.

He didn't know how to go about it and had never seen a dead person in that condition. But he had sewed sacks on the combine during wheat harvest. So he used the same system on the poor dead woman. When the supervisor came back, he said, "You did a great job! Where did you learn?"

"Well, I just used the same system I used on my dad's combine on the farm."

When a friend of his mother's in San Diego told him about a job at the vegetarian cafeteria, he was happy to leave the orderly job.

My friend, Annetta Rassmusen, in Salem, had a sister at Paradise Valley Sanitarium. Her husband, Glenn Bolten, was a doctor there. They told us to come on down, they would help us find work at the Sanitarium. Quentin decided to go, too. Pop Logan let us take their car, and we drove down together.

Ken was eagerly waiting my arrival, and the long trip down seemed like it would never end. Soon I would see the man I loved and had promised to marry.

Chapter 40

My Sweet Angel

It was a great weekend. Arriving in San Diego on Friday we found the Vegetarian Restaurant and Ken was waiting tables. Not the best place for a reunion! But we arranged to meet him after he finished work. He had made arrangements for us to all go to Balboa Park on Sabbath afternoon.

We all found jobs at the Sanitarium. Annetta and I stayed with her sister and brother in law. I liked my work. It consisted of answering the lights in the Sanitarium, where the more permanent patients were kept. I even wondered if maybe I should think of taking nursing. But, my looming marriage precluded that.

One day a light went on outside the door of room 377. When I went in, I found an older lady propped up, leaning on one arm. "Who are you?" she barked.

"My name is Alcyon, and I came to see if I can help you," I answered with a smile.

"Well, you look like you're good enough to wait on a pig!"

I was pretty non-plussed, but decided not to let her buffalo me. "Let's see, do you need some water? Here, let me fix your pillows so you'll be more comfortable," and I patted her shoulder.

She just stared at me. "Fix that curtain!" she ordered. "It's too low. No! Not that high!"

"Is that better?" I asked her as sweetly as I knew how. Finally, she agreed, "I guess it's OK now," and turned her face away with a scowl.

When I went out into the hall, some other nurses there were laughing. "So you found out about number 377. What happened?"

I just laughed and told them what she had said. From then on, those girls would try to be sure that I took light No. 377. I tried to never go in there without a smile, and treated the old lady as nicely as I could.

One day, when I walked in, she asked me to adjust her pillows. As I bent over her, she said, in a harsh voice, "Pretty girl!"

I almost asked her what she said. I couldn't believe it. From then on, she wasn't really nice, but she was never insulting again, and she would send the other girls out, asking for me.

I wondered what in the world had soured the poor old lady to that extreme. It was really fun to try to brighten her day.

Ken found another job that paid more. It was much harder work, on a dairy owned by a woman. She had prize cows that were heavy milkers and he had to milk twenty cows by hand, morning and night. He had a helper, and they lived together in a rustic cabin on the place.

The hours were horrid, starting at 4:00 A.M. Sometimes when he came to visit me, he almost fell asleep on the daveno as we visited. He would come after the afternoon milking. It was hard to pull away and sometimes he stayed so late there was little time to sleep before the next milking. One morning he over-slept and they had a hard time getting the milking done before the truck came for the milk.

He began to put the alarm clock right by his head on the nightstand. But then, he slept through the ringing. He would automatically reach over and turn it off and then fall asleep again. He tried another plan. He put a big dishpan upside down right by the bed with the clock on top so it would really make a racket. But, after a few days that plan failed also. Finally, he rigged up a string, hanging it from the ceiling, and tied it to the button at the top of the clock that had to be pushed down to turn off the alarm. That way the alarm wouldn't go off.

I hadn't heard from him for a few days, and one morning his helper at the farm called me. "Alcyon, Ken is real sick, almost out of his head. Can you come?"

I took the directions from him and went to La Jolla where the farm was. I had to walk into the place, but finally found it. I had taken some towels with me, because I was sure he would need some hot packs. After all, I had learned the Battle Creek method from my father.

When I walked in, I was horrified. The room was in a mess. Dishes hadn't been washed. The place was dirty, and there were literally thousands of flies. Ken was burning with fever, and barely conscious. I got the other fellow to help me get rid of the flies and clean up the place, while I heated water, and began to put hot packs on Ken's back. I kept on until his forehead became damp, and he was sweating. I knew that would bring down the fever. Then I did the same thing to his chest.

Soon, he looked at me, "How did you get here? I'm so glad to see you!"

Putting cold on his forehead, I explained how his friend had called me. "Why didn't you call me sooner?"

"I thought I would get better."

I stayed all day, giving him more treatments. I cooked up some food for them and gave him some hot soup. By evening his fever was down, but I told him, "The doctor's orders are that you stay in bed. I'll come back tomorrow."

As I went to go, he grabbed my hand, "You are my sweet angel. I'm so glad you came." I kissed his cheek and left.

The next day he was much better, and with some more treatments, I declared my patient well enough to be on his own. Telling him goodbye, he still insisted. "My darling, you really are my sweet angel." Those words rang in my ears all the way back to Paradise Valley.

Chapter 41

The Date Is Set

The next time Ken came to visit, he read me a letter from his parents. "There is a job opening to drive a route for the bakery in Longview."

We had a long discussion about our future plans. Then he asked, "What would you think about setting a date and getting married this spring?"

"Maybe it is time," I answered.

Before he left that day, we decided on a date for our wedding, June 22, 1941. When he kissed me goodbye, I was sad for him to leave, but excited to know that I would be starting to plan for our big day. It would be in the Salem church, the one where I grew up.

I began planning my wedding in earnest. Just like any girl in love, that wedding would be the high light of my life. By the time I went home a month later, I had the picture of the dress that I wanted, and I had our wedding planned to the last detail

Quentin decided to stay on at Paradise Valley longer, so I took the bus home. It was wonderful to be back with the family again, and Mom and I had so much to talk about. She would make my dress and help me with all my plans.

Ken came down the first weekend. We were thrilled to be together again, and our wedding was the topic of interest.

"It doesn't seem possible that we will be married in a month," he told me. "And yet, it will be hard to wait that long!"

"I know. I can hardly wait, but there is a lot to do in a month."

It would be just four weeks until the wedding. We went over the list I had made. "By the way," Kenny remembered, "Mom sent word for you to tell her how many invitations she can plan on. She is already making up her list."

"Well, she can invite as many as she wants to the wedding, maybe by an announcement in your church, but I suppose we need to have a limit as to how many we should invite to the reception." We decided on two hundred altogether.

I knew I needed to work until the wedding. It was strawberry harvest, and that seemed like the best way to earn some money in the short time we had. I was determined to have a wedding to remember, even if I had to pick fruit to pay for it. So, early every morning, our family, all except my father, went to the berry fields.

Mom told me, "I'll pick on your ticket. We'll work on your dress evenings."

We picked hard and fast all day from sun up to sun down. When cherry harvest started, we worked in that. I was getting in good shape!

A young single fellow was picking in the same field. Soon he started dumping buckets of cherries into my box. However, after I told him I was getting married, the generosity stopped!

Ken came down most weekends, and we were writing every day in between. At our 50th wedding anniversary in 1991, our eldest son, Ron, got into my old letters, and since he was the Emcee, he read some that we wrote that week! At least he knew and always did know that his parents were madly in love.

At that time there was only a piano in the Salem church. One day Pop told me, "You can't have a church wedding without an organ."

He arranged to rent one from a music company, and we asked my former organ teacher, William, to play.

When Pop found out I was only going to have cake and punch at the reception, he thought we should have ice cream, and ordered it. Of course, I asked him to take me up the aisle.

LaBreta was only nine, too big for a flower girl, but my only sister, and I wanted her in the wedding. She would be a junior bridesmaid. Wayne would help usher. Ken's mom knew I was working hard to pay for the wedding and wanted to help me, but I assured her, "No, we'll make it. Thank you anyway. This is something I want to do."

Enid couldn't come, so Annetta, would be my maid of honor. Jean and Mary Oliver would be bridesmaids.

Annetta suggested, "My sister, Dorothy, is good with flowers. She'll come and help me do the bridesmaids' bouquets."

Uncle Jess in Falls City, who had a nursery farm, sent word, "Don't worry about your flowers. I'll send a washtub full of Easter Lilies." I was ecstatic!

Quentin would go to Falls City to find mountain fern and bring the lilies. Everyone was helping. We were counting the days and then the hours. I had lots to do to get ready, but everything was going as scheduled. My two aunts and their families were coming from California.

My cousin, Bert Young, with a beautiful baritone voice would sing. A friend from Portland, would play the violin.

We rented the Carrier room in the large Methodist church in the center of town for the reception. Its steeple dominated the landscape, the oldest church in town, and the one where Mrs. White had spoken to a large audience on temperance.

My mother's father, Grandpa Johnson, an Adventist minister, was now old, and widowed, but he drove down from Ferndale, Washington for the event. Could it be possible? I was going to be a bride and all my family and friends were helping me. I would have a wedding to remember even if I had to pick fruit to pay for it!

Chapter 42

That Day In June

I woke to a bright Sunday morning in my upstairs bedroom. We had been up late the night before, attending to last minute details. Then it hit me, "This is my wedding day!" I looked over to the closet door, where my beautiful dress was hanging. It was a white organza with embroidered flowers, white on white.

I knew that my mother had put her love into every little detail of my dress, making it, perhaps, her crowning creation up to that time.

Odors of food wafted up the stairwell. Mom was already serving breakfast to the family and the relatives, who had arrived. Her two sisters were there, helping to make the sheet cakes for the reception. I had ordered the wedding cake.

It was time to get up. I had a long list to go through before the wedding that evening. But, I lingered a little longer. *This is my last day in my childhood home as a single girl. That is really a sobering thought! But I don't have any second thoughts. I have known since the night he proposed to me that he is the only man I have ever or will ever love. Tonight I will become his wife. Tomorrow will be a new world for me.*

I slipped into a dress and went down the stairs. As I neared the bottom, there was a cry, "Here comes the bride!" My loved ones were all there to share this day with me. I would love every minute of it.

"Alcyon, come and eat. You need a good breakfast today!" Aunt Dorothy was an efficient take-charge person, just older in the family than my mother. She would be a lot of help that day.

"Well, I can't say I'm hungry, but I appreciate all your concern!" And I sat down at the place they had prepared for me. I looked at my watch. "I need to hurry. Annetta and Mary will be at the church to help me decorate. I hope we have it finished before time for the rehearsal. Kenny will be coming about ten."

"Quentin left early to get the ferns and lilies," Mom told me. "He should be back by the time you are ready for them at the church."

When I finished eating, my two cousins, Kenny Kindopp and Bert Young, were ready to take me to the church. The girls were already there arranging the platform, the palm plants, candelabras, and ribbons on the aisle seats. The technicians were there installing the organ.

Quentin soon arrived with the ferns and lilies. They were waiting for me to arrange the platform. "Where are the tacks to fasten down the ribbons on the pews?" Annetta asked.

"Oh, I'm afraid I forgot to buy any. I'll run down to the store at the corner. Maybe they will have them," I said, heading for the door.

Thankfully, I found the tacks, and was walking back to the church when Ken and his family drove up. I glanced at my watch. "Ten o'clock on the dot!"

They parked across the street in front of the church. Ken had been driving, and stepped out. I hurried toward him and soon found myself in his arms.

The car was full of people and presents. There were Ken's parents, Grandma Lashier, and Jean. As Ken,

Jean and I walked into the church, he said, "This is beautiful! You have done a tremendous job."

When everyone came to greet him Annetta told us, "The organ technician was on the porch when Kenny drove up. When he came back in he announced, 'I think the groom just arrived, at least I hope he's the groom!' " Ken laughed, giving me another hug.

Someone announced, "I think the preacher is here."

Ken and I went to meet Elder Dickinson. Ken had worked with him in Evangelism. Soon we were ready for the rehearsal. Quentin went home to bring LaBreta and my father. William was already there, warming up the organ and setting up the stops.

In the rehearsal, Pastor Dickinson was informing us about the procedure. At a certain point, which would be the end of the pronouncement of man and wife, he said, "Now this is where you, uh, that is, if you want to—"

The pastor was a reserved type, but Ken understood and said, "Yes, we want to kiss!" The pastor was embarrassed to the amusement of the rest of us.

With the rehearsal over, Ken and I stood at the back, surveying the platform. I was overwhelmed with it all. "It is just beautiful. Everyone has been so great!"

Ken turned to me, "If there is nothing more I can do, I'll go and get ready." Then he held me close, "Until tonight, my darling. The next time I see you, you will be coming down the aisle!"

Back home, Mom and her sisters were insistent that I sit down and eat something, and then sent me upstairs to rest. It was a relief to be in my room alone for a little while, but sleep was far from me.

My heart went up to God, "Dear Father in Heaven. Thank you for the peace in my heart. Thank you for hearing and answering my prayers, and thank you for the gift of a Christian husband. I will be the best wife I can, and I will be faithful to him all the rest of my life."

At last we were at the church. We were waiting in the mother's room for the signal when the march would begin. I looked through the window into the sanctuary. That large church was filled to capacity. It seemed that the whole Longview congregation had come, as well as all of my fellow members. That show of affection for us almost brought tears to my eyes.

I looked to the front of the church. *It is so beautiful!* I thought. The rostrum was filled with baskets of Regal Easter Lilies, and another huge bouquet sat in the center of the choir railing. Baskets of mountain fern lined the front of the rostrum, with the candelabra and white candles forming a bower in the center.

William was at the organ with the rich music filling the church. When the minister walked on the platform, Ken was close behind. Wendell, the best man and Quentin and Forrest Roper, the groomsmen, followed. I was watching closely. *There he is! That man will soon be my husband!*

Then the coordinator started the procession with the bridesmaids, maid of honor and LaBreta with a little blue net dress just like the bridesmaids. My father was waiting, and I could see he was nervous. I had never thought of him as a nervous type, but as I took his arm and started up the aisle, he was literally shaking! I couldn't know the thoughts that crowded his mind, but I did see some tears in his eyes.

The church seemed to be filled with the fragrance of all those lilies. Then, we were at the foot of the steps. Ken was there to take my arm, and we walked up onto the platform together.

"Oh Promise Me" came through the rich tones of the violin. Everything seemed to be going in slow motion, but actually, I soon heard the minister speaking. "Beloved, we are gathered here today to join in holy matrimony this man and this woman."

Near the end of his remarks he used the text found in Ruth. "Entreat me not to leave thee, or to return from following after thee: for whither thou goest, I will go; and where thou lodgest I will lodge: thy people shall be my people, and thy God my God. Where thou diest, will I die, and there will I be buried; the Lord do so to me, and more also, if ought but death part thee and me."

Finally, the minister said, "I now pronounce this man, Kenneth Fleck, and this woman, Alcyon Logan, to be husband and wife. 'What God hath joined together let not man put asunder.'"

During our engagement days Ken would smile at me, and say, "I think we need to practice for that kiss at our wedding." But this wasn't a practice, it was the real thing. My husband was kissing me for the first time as his wife. I'm not sure if all the practicing helped any!

Bert sang, "My Heart is a Haven". And then the processional began. When we reached the lobby, we were to go to the basement, and from there to the Methodist church for the reception. As we started down the stairs, Ken reached his arm around my waist, and carried me all the way down!

When we arrived at the Carrier Room at the large Methodist church, we found the hall beautifully decorated with loads of flowers. We hadn't known that there would be another wedding there that afternoon. Their decorations were still there, along with ours from the church.

After the reception line of over 200 guests, Pastor Dickinson made an announcement that we had not planned. "There has been a request for the groom to sing to his bride, and for her to accompany him at the piano."

We looked at each other in surprise, but Ken said, "Come on, we can do it!" We knew the words and music to that song, so I sat at the grand piano with my husband standing nearby, and he sang, "I Love You Truly".

We headed to Rockaway, where Ken first wrote, **I Love You**, in the sand. That two-hour trip to the beach was unforgettable. The aroma of my corsage filled the car. I sat close to my new husband as he told me again how much he loved me, and we both agreed that our love and our marriage were gifts from God. The words that were read by the minister that evening were ringing in our ears as we headed into our future, "Whither Thou Goest, I Will Go!"

Chapter 43

Honeymoon Cabin

"Oh! This is just beautiful! Look Ken! They have everything arranged! Can you believe it?"

We had returned from our honeymoon and just stepped into the little cabin that would be our home for the present. It was the same cabin that Ken and his folks moved into after the fire that destroyed their house. Only now, it was all renovated. It was small, just three rooms, but it was so cozy! Since it was on Mom and Dad Fleck's farm, they were there to welcome us home.

"Grandma came and helped us fix it up," Mom Fleck said. "She thought it needed that flower box in front of the window. She even planted the flowers."

"That sounds like Grandma," Ken observed.

"And this big armchair is one of her gifts to you, too," Dad added.

I knew that she had made us four quilts, so we would have plenty of bedding.

"And where did this daveno come from?" I asked.

"Well, we thought you needed something to sit on in your living area," Dad told us. "I guess you can call that a wedding gift from Mom and me."

Ken and I were speechless. There was even a kitchen table, and a small electric portable stove. Ken's folks brought most of our gifts home with them. My family had brought us with the rest of the gifts. We had used their car for our honeymoon.

The bed was spread with a beautiful chenille bedspread from Aunt Mamie and her children. They had picked berries to earn the money for it. I was ecstatic. I had my own little house. There were still presents to unwrap, 200 altogether. It seemed that we had everything we needed.

Monday morning Ken drove off to work in the bakery truck and I was left alone like a queen in her mansion. I arranged everything to my taste, and even filled every one of the sixteen vases with flowers. Mom Fleck had planted flowers everywhere and she told me, "Just go and help yourself to all you want!"

As he was leaving for work I asked Ken, "How can I go to town to get the groceries and things that I need?"

"Just take the old Durant. Here are the keys. And here is $10. Will that be enough?"

I knew that Ken had $200 in a sock on our honeymoon. We used half of it then, and the rest we saved to start housekeeping. It seemed like quite a lot to us.

After washing the dishes and putting the little house in order I prepared to go to town. I wasn't an experienced driver and had never driven the old Durant, but finally got the old thing going. It was fun, that first trip to shop as a married lady! I spent $5 to buy groceries and the other half to buy a broom, dishpan, etc. When Ken came home that evening he found the table set, and the best meal I knew how to prepare. "Welcome home, my dearest," I told him as he wrapped his arms around me.

We were as happy as if we were living in a mansion. There was even the old piano that Grandma and Uncle

Arthur had helped to pull out of the burning house. I loved playing it while Ken sang.

His parents always had a big garden. They must have planted extra that year. Wanting to prepare for winter I picked beans and took them to the custom cannery. As the different fruits and vegetables were ready I took advantage of them.

One morning Ken asked me, "Why don't you go with me on the route today? It would be lots more fun with you along."

"I would love to, just give me a few minutes to get ready. I'll make a picnic lunch for us."

We never tired of being together. There was so much to talk about. Our heads were full of ideas and plans for the future. The immediate goal was for Ken to finish his theology course, so we needed to save money for college. I thought I might take some classes too. That day we reveled in the reality of actually being married and all of the possibilities of our new life together.

But the honeymoon was over and serious decisions faced us. Our biggest concern was to get on with our plans for Ken to finish his education and get his degree in Theology. One evening, studying our finances, he voiced his concern. "I don't think we'll make it back to Walla Walla this next fall on this income."

We discussed various other possibilities. Threats of World War II dominated the news. Shipyards were being built in Vancouver and also Bremerton. People were moving to the West Coast from the middle and southern states to find work. He continued, "Do you think we should consider looking for work in one of the ship yards?"

"It would be hard to leave our little Honeymoon Cabin, but I know that our goals for the future have to be our priority. I suppose it is something to consider," I answered. "But we have such a cute little place here and your folks went to a lot of work to fix this little cabin for us."

"I know," he answered." But we have to face the fact that we could probably make a lot more if we went up to Bremerton where the main shipyards are. Maybe we should just go up and try it out. If things don't work out we can come back. I think they would still use me at the bakery."

We put the idea on the back burner deciding to look into the possibilities.

Chapter 44

Tragedy Strikes

Ken had just left for work one morning when his mom knocked at my door. "One of my friends has heard of pears that are a good price. I'm going to get some and take them to the custom cannery to do up. Would you like to take advantage and go with us?"

"Yes! I want to put up all the fruit I can. With war looming, prices may get higher. When are you leaving?"

"I still have to finish the dishes. It will be at least half an hour."

I had helped my mom can fruit since I was very young. It would be great to bring home a good supply of canned pears for our winter supply. We purchased the pears and found a place to work at the cannery. I had already finished one box and was on the next one, when the hired man from the farm came in looking for me.

"Alcyon, a call just came from your father in Salem. He said to tell you that Wayne was hurt seriously, a fractured skull, and is in the hospital. You should come home."

My heart raced. How could this have happened! Wayne was my precious little brother, the one I had helped to care for as a baby, and who had been close to me all those years. He had grown up to be a big handsome boy, now 13 years old. He had attended Junior High School that year and was especially interested in science. He even had a little chemistry lab in our basement.

Somehow we found Ken on his route and he came home. His Uncle Harold happened to be visiting the folks at that time, and he told Ken, "Take my car, it will get there faster." Soon we were on our way to Salem.

I noticed the speed indicator at over eighty miles an hour much of the time. Ken was going as fast as he dared, and we were praying earnestly. I remember telling him, as we neared the city limits of Salem, "Let's go to the house first. If the lights are all on, I'll know we are too late. If the house is dark we'll go to the hospital." No one will ever know how I dreaded to drive up to that house.

But we were too late. Every light in the house seemed to be on, and there were cars in front. The front door was open and I ran in. Even as I ran up the porch I could hear my mother wailing from the couch where she was lying. The minister's wife, Mrs. Ernston, was fanning her. Those moments are hard for me to write about, even now. I dropped to my knees wrapping my mother in my arms. "Oh Mama! I am so sorry!" My father was standing by weeping silently.

I had to forget my own grief and find a way to comfort my mother. She was saying, "I'm so glad you are here, Alcyon. He's gone! My little boy is gone. Oh! How can I bear it?"

I murmured into her ear. "But, Mama, he was always such a good boy. We'll see him again!"

Finally, Mom's first intense grief subsided and we began to talk. My father began to tell us about the accident. "He was over at Olinger field." That is a city playground by a river. "He was swimming, but had dressed and was on his way to come home, when he passed some friends who were riding bicycles over the teeter boards. He didn't have his bicycle that day, but he borrowed another boy's to try it. It seems that there was a loose spike that stuck up and it caused the bicycle to flip. Wayne landed in the gravel on his head." Pop could hardly finish telling us. "His head was fractured from the crown to down to his nose. He didn't have a chance. He only lived two hours."

How we lived through those terrible hours I will never know. Ken and I did all we could to bring comfort to my parents, and to help them with the arrangements that had to be made. The next day Ken went back to take care of his job, planning to come down for the funeral.

"Alcyon, will you please take care of Wayne's things?" my mom asked me. I went up to his room, doing what had to be done. I found his Bible on the nightstand and the Junior Bible Year Calendar beside it. He had marked off each chapter as he read it. The last chapter he read was Ecclesiastes 12. I turned the leaves of his Bible and found the first verse of that chapter, "Remember now thy Creator in the days of thy youth."

I took the Bible and ran down stairs. My parents were sitting in the living room with tear-stained faces. "Just listen to this. I checked his Bible Year Calendar. All the chapters were marked up through Eccl. 12." Then I read the first verse. "Doesn't that give you comfort?"

"Yes, it does. I know he was ready. He was a good boy," my mother said.

Then Pop added, "You know, he hadn't been baptized, but he was preparing for it."

Later that day an old friend came to visit us, Mrs. Sundin. She was older with grown children. Although her husband was not a Christian she seemed like a true saint, a quiet, sweet little lady whom I had known ever since moving to Salem.

She began, "Sister Logan, I want to tell you something. I had a son, a beautiful boy that I adored after having three girls. He was drowned. My grief was so deep I could not give him up. I prayed, literally demanding that God bring him back. When the efforts to revive him seemed in vain, and every one else gave up, I still prayed on. You know, the Lord answered, and he revived. But I have lived to regret that prayer. My son died in a drunkard's grave. How I wish that I had let him go when he was young and innocent. Your boy is safe in God's hands. Don't grieve as those who have no hope. And trust God that He knows what is best. You can have your boy with you again, but I can't."

That visit did bring comfort to all of us, and I never forgot it. In the years when I was a pastor's wife and a missionary, I tried to bring comfort to the grieving many times. I knew that in this world, death is hard to face, but it is wonderful to be able to look beyond the grave and know there will be a resurrection!

My older brother, Quentin, was working in Bremerton, and it was hard to get the word to him. But he was able to come in time for the funeral. I know that he, too, suffered keenly the loss of his little brother.

The night before the funeral, Ken was back and we all went to the mortuary to see Wayne. He was such a beautiful boy, but his head was misshapen from the terrible injury. He was in the new suit he had just bought to wear to our wedding. I hadn't seen him since then. His death brought a shadow to our lives in spite of the happiness in our new life together. I prayed for healing from that blow to my parents and also for the rest of us. For months afterwards, the horror of

Wayne's death haunted my dreams and I would wake up in a sweat. But, eventually time does heal, and we began to think more of the wonderful day when that shout from heaven will release God's sleeping saints from their graves. Ken and I were all the more determined to dedicate our lives to spreading that wonderful news.

Chapter 45

Planes In The Fog!

That fall Ken found a job at the shipyards in Bremerton. We hated to leave our cozy cabin, but we wanted to be in college by the next fall. That would take some doing.

At first we lived in a house trailer that Ken and a relative pulled up to Bremerton. The parks were full of people working in the shipyards. We found a spot to park the trailer and Ken began to work. It was a miserable job out on the dock in the cold, rainy weather. He worked on the tide shift. They were doing repair under the dock and had to work when the tide was out, an hour later each night.

I told Ken some rather unexpected news one day. "It looks like you are going to be a father!"

"Really! Wow! That is unexpected news!" He took me in his arms. "You will be a wonderful mother, and I will be a proud and happy father."

"But what about our finances and our plans for college?" I asked.

"Well, we'll have to tighten our belts a little more. But don't you worry about it. The main thing will be that you are OK and that we have a healthy baby. We'll find a way, and still get to Walla Walla next fall."

When Grandma Lashier heard the news, she had a positive perspective. "That's wonderful! People should have their children when they are young."

Our parents also took an optimistic view. Mom Fleck's response was, "This will be the first grandchild on both sides of your families. That is like Kenneth was, and somehow it gives a child a special place in the family. I will be thrilled to be a grandma."

My father had a big smile, but didn't say much, and Mom was happy. "I love babies, and this one will be welcomed with open arms."

The trailer was hard to heat and not the best place for a young expectant mother who had morning sickness! We finally found a cabin out at a small community, called Happy Hollow, on the Hood Canal. When I first saw it I told Ken, "It isn't fancy, but it will be a lot better than the trailer. At least we can keep warm with this big old cook stove."

Our cabin was just a few feet from the water near a general store. There were two rooms, a bedroom and kitchen and living combined. We borrowed a trailer and brought our furniture from Longview. The daveno barely fit in, but it made us more comfortable. It was a 30 minute drive in to Bremerton in the old Durant, but longer by bus, which Ken usually used.

We hadn't been living there long when Ken came back from the store one morning with the startling news, **Pearl Harbor has been attacked by Japanese planes!** There were huge headlines on the front page of the paper."

"Oh no! What will happen now? Are we in danger?"

Ken was home since he was working the tide shift. We went outside and looked across the canal toward the Pacific just beyond. It was a dark, foggy day and planes droned overhead. When it came over the news that Japanese planes had been sighted off the coast, each time we heard a plane, I would ask, "Could that be Japanese?"

Because of the fog we couldn't see, only hear them. That went on for hours. Ken tried to assure me, "We are probably hearing Navy planes, patrolling the coast."

It was a serious, uncertain time. Everyone wondered if the west coast would be attacked next, and especially the shipyards. People were keeping their ears glued to radios to catch the latest news.

When we heard that Japanese ships had been spotted off the coast, that was further cause for alarm. What should we expect? Did we make a mistake to move to Bremerton? Finally, it seemed there was no immediate danger and, little by little, things settled down to a state of alert, but one we could live with.

While the little cabin was an answer to our housing problem at first, Ken began to realize that the distance to his job made the days too long. I was alone out there trying to keep the fire going, chopping wood if I ran out, and waiting for him to come home.

One day he suggested, "Why don't we go into town and see if we can find an apartment to rent?"

"That's a wonderful idea! Can we go today?"

"Yes, I don't have to work until six tonight. Let's see what we can find."

I was happy for his suggestion and it didn't take me long to get ready. We heard of an apartment in a residential area of town that was within our budget. As soon as I walked in I exclaimed, "This is perfect for us. Look at the cute little kitchen!"

And as soon as we could make arrangements we moved in. It wasn't much bigger but did have modern conveniences. I liked the little apartment. We had all our earthly belongings there and I soon had it all arranged to suit me.

As the Christmas season neared, we were nostalgic about the holiday and wanted to make this first Christmas of our married life something special. I thought that a little tree on our table with a string of blue lights would be romantic. We both went shopping, spending our entire budget for that month on presents for each other. As Christmas neared, we had our little tree all set up with the carefully wrapped presents around it.

But when December 24 came along, suddenly we both got a lonesome feeling. "You know," Ken ventured, " we could be there by supper time if we left within the hour. What do you think?"

"I think it would be fun. Let's go!"

"Let's just pack up the old Durant and go home. We could have Christmas Eve tonight in Longview and go down to Salem tomorrow for Christmas Day."

"What about our presents?" I asked.

"Let's just box them up and take them along."

Soon we were on our way. As we rode along the long December night set in, and we watched for the few displays of Christmas lights we could see. Because of the war there was an energy alert and people were encouraged to forgo Christmas lights. But we were going home!

Ken's folks were surprised and delighted to see us. Grandma Lashier was there, as well as Ken's sister, Jean, and also his Aunt Alice. When they opened the presents we were surprised that there were packages for us, too.

I whispered to Ken. "This is embarrassing. We didn't bring them any presents."

We didn't have any presents for anyone but ourselves. Our presents all said, To Kenneth from Alcyon, or To Alcyon from Kenneth!

When we went to Salem the next day Mom met us at the door with a big smile and hugs. We were in time for Christmas dinner, but again we didn't have any presents to bring. It was a little hard to explain, but it did furnish a comical memory for us when we remembered our First Christmas!

Chapter 46

War Years

Ken worked his changing shifts, coming home at all hours. Although dressed in the appropriate clothing for working, sometimes, in the water, it was a cold, hard job. My role was to keep the home fires burning, make good, nourishing lunches for him, and the best meals I knew how to make.

Quentin was working on the docks, too, and moved in with us. We considered we were a part of the war effort, doing the best possible under the circumstances. I was still plagued with morning, and sometimes evening, sickness, but knew that, even so, my role was much easier than theirs.

The fellows began talking of other alternatives for making money, but it was mostly dreaming, not really planning to make a change.

One evening when they were both home Quentin came up with an idea. "Our cousin, Clyde Sample, in Falls City is logging up in the mountains near Valsetz. He told me there is plenty of timber up there. Maybe we could go up there and cut firewood and haul it into Salem to sell."

"Maybe we could find an old army truck to haul it with," Ken suggested.

Ken came home one day with bad news. "Because of the urgency of the war, there will be seven day shifts from now and no special favors."

"What does that mean?" I asked.

"It means that Quentin and I will no longer have Sabbaths free. I talked to our supervisor today. There's nothing he can do. Plenty of people are waiting for the job."

Now the wood cutting business became more interesting. Finally, he and Quentin decided to go to Falls City, talk to Clyde, and see if they could swing it. We decided to keep our apartment for the time being while they investigated the new venture. I would stay with my parents in Salem until their plans were final.

They came back, full of enthusiasm. They would be woodsmen and make a lot of money! "What about me?" I asked. "Where will we live?"

"Well," Ken hesitated, "You could stay with your folks in Salem. But we really need a cook. We plan to get a tent and camp."

"You don't need to think you are going to leave me in Salem," I laughed. "I like to camp."

We ended up with a tent, large enough for a bed, and a makeshift kitchen and a little wood stove to cook on. I was the cook. Even though, our baby would be arriving in a couple of months, I was excited about the possibilities. I loved the mountains and outdoors. Whenever a tree was about to be felled they would call me to come and watch.

Just as the big giant was ready to fall, they would yell, **"TIMBER!"** And it would crash, making the ground shake.

They did cut a lot of wood and they sold what they cut in town. But there were complications. The old truck didn't always perform and, of course, they didn't have any capital for repairs.

One day Ken heard from his parents, "We have heard of a job available in the Long Bell mill that would be good pay and more reliable than the wood cutting business." They added, "You remember the big house back down the road behind our place that the Ziesmans used to have. It is empty and you can rent it."

Ken looked at me, "Being the cook up in the mountains probably isn't the best place for you as the baby's arrival date is nearing. What do you think?"

"Well, it's been fun in the mountains, but I think it is probably the part of wisdom to go to Longview."

The wood business ended, and we went back to Longview, just in time, because Ronald Wayne arrived before we had even moved into the old house.

Ken's Grandma Lashier still lived alone in her house in Meadow Glade, and as she told it, "Kenneth came all excited. 'Grandma. We have a baby boy and he is just beautiful!' I have never seen that boy so excited."

Grandma, who was 75 years old then, offered to go with Kenneth with his parents' car, pulling a trailer, to bring our furniture from Bremerton. In those days, they kept new mothers in bed for ten days. By that time Mom Logan and Grandma Lashier had cleaned up the old house, hung curtains and arranged our furniture.

The first day that I was alone in my house with my new baby was unforgettable. Ken was at work. I was sitting in a rocking chair by an open window, holding little Ronnie in my arms. The lace curtain was blowing gently in the breeze. I savored the moment, This is my home and this is my baby. My happiness was so deep and so complete that the tears rolled down my cheeks. I lifted my heart to God, "Oh, thank you, Lord! Thank you for this precious gift, this child You have given us. Help me to be a good mother and a good wife, and please guide us in our future. We will go wherever You lead."

It would be the last big push to get our finances in order; Ken's old school bill paid, and be ready for him to be back in College that fall for his last two years of Theology. He began working at the mill. Soon they gave him two extra nights of work.

Then Dad Fleck told him, "There is plenty of pasture down at your place. If you are interested, I'll loan you eight of our milk cows, and you can have the milk to sell to the creamery." It was always Dad's policy to let us make our way, but help us to do that at times.

It was the last of May and we were determined to make our goal of being in Walla Walla for the coming quarter in October.

That summer Ken's sister, Jean, married Don Duncan. They had inherited our honeymoon cabin and were also working hard to be in College that fall. Don was on the same schedule at the mill.

Those four months were a trial to our faith, but God somehow helped us through. Ken was working the long hard eight-hour shifts at the mill, besides two extra nights a week. He needed to milk the cows early in the morning, get the cans of milk ready to take to the creamery with Dad's cans, and then repeat the process at night. Finally, he sent for his young cousin, Glenn, about 12 years old, to come and help him.

With the new baby, keeping house and cooking, I was busy too. But one day I got sick. I was chilling, and my temperature spiked up to 105 degrees in a few hours. The doctor came, deciding there was an infection. Mom Logan came to take care of me and the baby.

But the work program had to go on for Ken. Those were some of the hardest days of his life. It took weeks for me to get my strength back. We were still determined to reach our goal of being in Walla Walla when school started. God gave Ken the strength to do what he had to do. I survived the health crisis, and the end of the summer found us with our finances in order to begin the next step toward our dream.

Chapter 47

College at Last

Ken came home with the letter we were waiting for. "Good news!" he announced. "We have a house in College Place ready to move into!"

"Tell me about it. I can't wait!" This was the last problem to be solved, a place to live while Ken started his junior year in Theology.

"It is a little house just a block or so behind Conard Hall. It is partly furnished and with what we have will be enough. And the rent is within our budget."

"Wonderful!" I answered. "I will be so glad to actually be in College Place and in a real house."

I would be busy taking care of baby Ronnie and keeping house. Also, we hoped to arrange for some classes in music for me. For now, any further progress in my education would have to wait.

Our furniture would be sent on a truck and the rest would have to fit in the Model T truck that Ken purchased for $25 that had taken the place of the old Durant. It wasn't really a truck, but someone had built a box on the back. There was no money to buy a better car. We just hoped the old truck would get us to College Place.

With everything already packed in the truck except the things we would need on the way, we spent the last night at Mom and Dad Fleck's. Diapers were drying around the house, and early in the morning we were all in. There was canned food that our parents had contributed, all our personal things, and Ronnie's baby buggy. The baby equipment I would need on the way was tucked in around my feet in the front seat. Four-month's old Ronnie was in my arms. We were crowded but happy. Everyone was out waving to us as we chugged down the lane to the main road.

We were thrilled to finally be on our way. But soon after getting on to the highway leading to Portland, there was an ominous noise in the engine. Ken pulled over to a nearby gas station. Soon he came around to my side, "Bad news! Lizzie has given up. I don't think she is going another step!"

"What will we do?" I almost panicked.

"I'll have to call the folks," Ken said. "Uncle Harold is there. I think he will come and help us." He soon came with his new car, loaded us all in and took us on to Walla Walla.

It was a bad start, but we had the optimism of youth. We found another antique car, this time a Model A Ford that cost $35. That car would last for the two years until Ken graduated. The little house was cozy. Ken took a full load that year besides finding odd jobs to bring in extra money to help with our expenses.

There was a wood range in the kitchen that we cooked on. I baked our bread, but one day Ken suggested, "Why don't you bake enough to last?"

My reasoning didn't satisfy him, so I suggested, tongue in cheek, "Why don't you bake bread?" He wasn't known for his cooking expertise.

"Don't you think I can do it?" he asked.

"Well, maybe you can show me that you can," never dreaming he would try.

The next day he came home from classes, went to the kitchen and began his preparation for making bread. He found a recipe some place, got out a huge pan and began mixing a double recipe! When I finally got the baby to bed that night, Ken was still in the kitchen mixing his bread, letting it rise and kneading it down. He was stoking the stove to get the oven hot enough when I went to bed.

In the morning I found twelve beautiful loaves of bread on the counter. "Well, you proved you could do it!" I told him. And it was great bread!

By Christmas time, the owners decided to move into their house and we found a nice little basement apartment in what was called the Repp's house. There were two other college couples, one in the apartment across from us in the basement and another in the attic.

Mother and Dad Repp were surrogate parents to all of us young couples. They were German with the typical accent and called us 'the chillun'. To my great joy there was an upright piano in the little living room of our apartment.

One day Mother Repp told us, "You just put your baby to bed at night when you need to go out. Our bedroom is right above your apartment and I can watch him."

She also told us, "We just love to lie in bed and listen to the music coming from your apartment." Ken sang in a quartet and we often had groups in to practice.

Ken found a job as night watchman at the college. He was able to do his studying between making his rounds. When his grades came out with all A's but one he decided that being married had definitely improved his scholarship!

Jean and Don were back at college, too, living in an apartment in the village. We spent many of our recreational times with them. Jean hadn't missed any years in her college days and would graduate the same time as Ken.

At the end of the first year, we knew we needed to find a way to earn extra money for his senior year. There was an opening at the Marvel Bakery in Portland for retail truck drivers. It was in the midst of the war years with people from all over the country working in the shipyards in Vancouver. There was special housing for them where everyone of age in the family would be working. The bakery trucks drove through those housing projects to deliver bread and other bakery goods. We found a place to live in Portland, and he drove long hours delivering bread. We would make it another year, and then our primary goal would be reached.

By Christmas of the second year, funds were getting low. Ken wrote to the route manager of the bakery to see if they might have a temporary job for him during the Christmas break. We were excited when the answer came. "Actually, we have two drivers wanting to take their vacation. If you and Alcyon want to do it, you can each take a route."

Ken looked at me, "What do you think? Do you want to try it?"

I had been driving a lot, even the old Model T and now the Model A. "Sure, I've gone with you on the routes. I think I could do it. But what about Ronnie and where would we stay?"

"Well, we could stay out at Meadow Glade with Grandma Lashier, I think. We would have to drive back and forth every day to Portland."

Then I added, "I'm sure my mom would take care of Ronnie and we could go down there on weekends." Mom Logan was a natural with babies and she loved to have Ronnie with her. I knew she would welcome the idea.

The two-week break found us at Grandma Lashier's, living in her attic bedroom. At 5:00 A.M. every morning we would go down to a wonderful breakfast and come home to a bountiful supper, usually at 9:00 P.M. Ken's route took him one direction and mine was out to Forest Grove and Hillsboro, a ninety-mile route every day.

We loaded our trucks in the morning and met back at the bakery in the evening to drive home together. One morning we woke up to a white world. "Oh no!" I exclaimed. "I've never driven in the snow, much less a panel." The thought of driving ninety miles through snow in and out of farm roads was a daunting prospect.

"You'll make it," Ken assured me. "Just take it easy, and don't brake too fast if you start to slide."

God gave me courage and safety, and I praised him when I saw other cars in the ditch, but I never got stuck, even backing around people's farmyards.

Ken was making $20 a day and I was making $15. By staying an extra week and going back to school late we saved enough to take us to the end of the school year and Ken's graduation. Back in our apartment, we reviewed the bakery venture. "I didn't know I could do it," I told Ken. "But God has blessed us with the funds we need to make it through."

"Yes, we can thank Him for that," Ken added. "You were a trouper."

Those last two quarters were busy ones but also meaningful for us. In Ken's Homiletics class we were assigned to conduct meetings at a little church in Wallula on weekends. We made a bed in the back seat of the car where Ronnie could nap and we spent the whole day Sabbath there, with visiting in the afternoons and a meeting at night. I was the pianist and Ken and another young Theology student took turns preaching and leading the music.

"You know, Ken, this is like it will be in the ministry. I already feel like a pastor's wife!"

As graduation time drew near we were wondering about our future. "There are more graduates from Theology this year than usual," Ken told me one day. "It is pretty certain that many of us won't get calls."

"What will we do if we don't get a call?" I asked.

"That's a good question. I think we need to pray about it."

"Well, God has been leading us and helping us so far. Let's just leave it in His hands."

Then one day he came rushing in from school. "I have news! We are going to have visitors!"

"Whoever would that be?" I asked, noticing his excitement.

"I met Elder Belleau, who is the president of the Idaho Conference, today. He asked if he and the treasurer, Elder Hagen, could come to see us! They will be here at 2:00, and that isn't very long from now."

Looking at the clock, I agreed. "No, it is 12:30 now. Well, dinner is ready. Let's eat right away so I can have everything cleaned up before they come!"

At two o'clock sharp there was a knock at our door. Two well-dressed men stood there. Ken hurried to open it, and Elders Belleou and Hagen came in.

Elder Belleau walked over and threw his hat on top of the piano. Without any preliminaries he turned to us, "How would you like to come to Idaho?"

Our hearts nearly stopped! We had wondered, *Would we get a call after all the struggle of getting the preparation?*

Ken, taken by surprise, replied, "Well, have a seat," motioning to the daveno, "and tell us more about it."

We learned that Elder Belleau didn't waste words. "Elder John Trude, pastor and evangelist of the Blackfoot district, is going to hold meetings in a tent. We need an associate for him and a song leader and pianist. We understand that you folks fill the bill."

Needless to say, we didn't need to think about it. We had been praying earnestly for God's direction in our future. Ken looked at me and then answered, "I think we would be delighted to come to your conference."

They went on to talk about the details, the conference truck that would come for our furniture, and when we would be expected to arrive. Elder Belleau was very explicit. "I would like for you to be in Boise and meet Elder Trude at the corner of (two intersecting streets) at 2:00 P.M., and he gave us the specific date. We knew then that we would be working for a president who knew exactly what he expected from us.

Then he asked us about our car situation.

Ken laughed and replied, "If you looked out back you would see a Model A Ford. That is all we could afford and stay in school."

The president looked at his treasurer and Elder Hagen told us, "We have a policy of advancing a down payment for a car to our workers. I'm sure we can arrange this."

After a prayer the two pastors left, and we sat on the sofa stunned. Ken broke the silence. "We have a job and we have our marching orders." We both laughed and agreed that that call from God was pretty definite and we would do our best.

Graduation weekend arrived. Mom and Dad Fleck came as both of their children were graduating. Strangely, I had no thoughts of disappointment that it wasn't me graduating. Ken and I were one. His success was mine and I sat in the audience with little two-year-old Ronnie on my lap feeling a happiness that brought tears to my eyes. *From now on, my role will be to stand by my husband's side and support him in every way I can. I am so proud to be his wife. God will be our leader.*

Chapter 48

A Dream Come True

It was a morning we would never forget. The conference truck had come and gone with all our belongings except those in our new car. It wasn't a new car, but one that seemed to fit our needs, a Mercury. We were on our way to our new role as workers in the Idaho Conference.

As we neared Boise, Ken remarked, "I wonder if Elder Trude will be on time at the corner Elder Belleau indicated."

"Well, if he has been working under Elder Belleau very long, I would guess that he will be there," I answered with a smile.

Before we knew it we were driving into the outskirts of Boise. We found the special corner, and sure enough a big, tall man dressed like a minister, was there waiting for us. We were right on time.

"I see you made it, and right on time," John laughed, greeting us warmly. "I guess you have an idea now about how our president operates!"

It was a pleasure to learn to know John and later his little wife, Thelma. We also met John's father who lived with them. Father Trude was another John in appearance, only showing the effect of years. From the start we knew that John was his pride and joy.

We found a little apartment in the house of an elderly lady in Blackfoot. It wasn't long before Ken and John were busy getting the tent ready for meetings.

Ken came in the door one day with the news, "It looks like you and I have our first project."

"What is that?" I asked. I didn't know that I was to be involved except to help in the meetings.

"John wants us to go to every house in this little town and do a survey of people's church affiliations, and religious preferences. Of course we will also invite them to the meetings."

"Oh, well, that is interesting. When do we begin?" *I was thinking, It's a good thing we brought LaBreta along for the summer. She will be baby-sitting Ronnie.*

From the start the meetings were well attended. John was a powerful speaker and both he and Ken kept busy visiting the interested people. Ken led the music, while I played. He sang solos each evening and sometimes he and John sang duets.

I had taken a class on chalk drawings so I put my questionable art talents to use by making chalk drawings with Ken singing and accompanying himself on the piano. One that people liked was of a hill, backed by the setting sun, and silhouetted with three crosses on the top. Ken sang all four verses of the beautiful song, "Calvary". People liked the simple drawings and Elder Trude offered them as prizes to those who brought the most guests. We often saw those rustic pictures hanging on people's walls as we visited them!

During the tent meetings, it was Ken's job to sleep in the tent to take care of all the equipment there. He had a cot he put up each night right beside the platform and usually placed his clothes right beside him on the platform.

One night he was sound asleep and woke up with a start, hearing someone talking right outside the tent. A man was mumbling. "I'll get ya'. I'll kill ya'!"

Petrified, he grabbed his clothes and crept on the sawdust to the back of the tent and then hurriedly dressed. Running around the block to the police station, he told them, "Come quick!" And then explained the problem.

An officer took him in his car back to the tent. Carefully shining his spotlight around behind the tent, again they heard the voice and the profanity. A closer look revealed a black man lying just inside the tent for shelter from the cold, apparently drunk.

As the officer pulled him into his wagon, the unfortunate man was saying. "I's leavin' in de mo'nen, boss. I's leavin' in de mo'nen!" Needless to say, Ken's sleep was not the best for the rest of that night.

The summer passed quickly and there was a good baptism. Then the conference asked us to go to the western side of Idaho in the Payette and Weiser district to help Elder Joe Apigian with another series of meetings. It was an experience to work with Elder Apigian. He was so dynamic that his shirt would be wet when he finished preaching.

When the Harvest Ingathering campaign started at Christmas time, we were delegated to do our part in Payette. Singing bands were organized. One Sabbath Ken and I had spent Sabbath at the church in Vale. Jean and Don, as well as another couple, Byron and Paloma Chalker, friends from college, were visiting us.

We had planned a different evening, but Elder Apigian called and instructed us to show up for singing bands. Kenneth thought he would take the fellows. I needed to get food ready for us and put our tired little Ronnie to bed. But that wasn't Elder Apigian's plan. He informed Ken, "My wife doesn't want to go either, but she has to go. We need Alcyon there too!"

We ended up taking our guests and making our own singing band. Paloma and I solicited, and we came back with around $80, which was a lot for those times. The six of us often talked about that Saturday night singing band, and we agreed it was a great time to remember. I had to admit that Elder Apigian was probably right!

After the meetings closed, Ken was assigned to pastor the northern part of the district where there was a church in Council. We found a little house behind the home of one of our members. We were also assigned to hold some meetings on our own in the small town of Midvale. That was a new experience.

We rented a hall on Main Street and prepared it for meetings. Some of our new friends from Weiser came the first Saturday night to help swell the crowd. Ken was the preacher, the song leader, the janitor who fed the wood stove in the corner, and I was the pianist and "artist" to do the chalk drawings. With all the advertising we thought the hall would be full, but, to our great disappointment, only a few stray people came in.

The next night was Sunday. No friends came, just Ken and I, but lo and behold, people began streaming in the door. Ken had to put up more chairs. The hall was filled with 63 people. That experience bolstered our faith. We thanked God for helping us.

Elder Apigian called one day during those meetings, "I was asked to have a funeral there in Midvale for an Adventist sister, who was an invalid. She is the only member we have in that little town. She is a pioneer, loved by everyone, and her funeral will be in the High

School. I have a conflict and can't make it, so you, Kenneth, will have to take my place."

When we learned that the funeral would be in the High School, Ken was nervous. It would be his first funeral, and there wouldn't be any other Adventists there. When we arrived at the High School people were pouring in and soon filled the large auditorium.

Ken met the funeral director and made himself known. Feeling insecure, he asked, "What is the order of service?"

The funeral director answered matter-of-factly, "Just whatever your custom is, Reverend."

I sat in the audience praying, but I never feared for Ken. I knew he could do it. God used him in a wonderful way as he spoke of Jesus Second Coming when the dead will arise to meet Him in the clouds.

At the interment his nervousness almost got to him. At the committal, he was reading out of the Pastor's Hand Book. "And now we commit this dear sister (or brother)—" realizing too late that he had included the words in parentheses!

In spite of all the trauma of that first funeral in his life as a pastor, Ken had the great joy of meeting the woman's son, who had strayed from his faith, but who knew that his mother's prayers had followed him. After that sermon on the soon coming of Jesus, that prodigal son came home.

Chapter 49

The Interlude

Our new district was spread out, all the way from Payette to McCall. What we had thought was a bargain on our Mercury turned out to be a major problem. It had a cracked head on the motor. This was devastating news for us. We owed the conference and the bank on it yet. We couldn't get along without a car, and yet we were determined not to go further into debt.

After much deliberation Ken asked for a leave of absence for a time. We hoped in that way to resolve the present indebtedness and get a car that would be paid for. After consultation with the conference they reluctantly agreed to our request.

At first Ken thought he would work in a lumber mill, but Dad Fleck had another idea. "The Meadow Glade Store at Columbia Academy is looking for a new owner."

The Academy owned the store, but the contents could be purchased and the building rented from the school. Actually, Ken's grandfather had built that store and operated it years before when the Academy was first begun. Business had always appealed to Ken, and when he suggested the idea to me I asked, "Where would we get the money to buy the stock?"

"I'll ask Dad if he would be willing to lend it to us. We should be able to start paying him back right away. It is a good neighborhood store."

In a short time I became the wife of a businessman instead of a pastor. We were disappointed, but felt it was the right thing to do instead of incurring more debt on a starting salary. Meadow Glade was home to Ken. He was born a mile or two away and his family was among the pioneers of that Adventist community. Grandma Lashier lived on the corner just a few steps away. There was a small house connected to the store where we would live.

Soon, Ken began to make that store a paying proposition. He was a natural people person, opened up credit accounts and even delivered groceries for older people. On Saturday nights he would open the store and it became a gathering place for people and students from across the street at the Academy.

One year went by and business was booming. The war was still raging, some items were hard to get and he would save them for his regular customers. There was a gas pump that kept busy when people had coupons for gas. I helped in the store when he went to Portland with his little truck to get supplies, and I learned to pump gas.

It was during that first year that we were expecting another baby. We had a real scare a few nights before the due date. I had a bad cough and got up to get some cough medicine but fell flat on my face.

Ken woke up to my screaming and came running. When he got me back in bed, the whole bed was shaking with my trembling. I was crying, "I've killed it! I've killed it!"

Mom Logan had lost her first baby by falling just a few days before the birth and the perfectly formed little girl was born dead. I was sure the same thing was happening to me.

For an hour or so there was no movement, but finally we knew she was still alive, but then worried about injury to the baby. But Carolyn Jean was born soon with no bad effects, and after examining her from head to toe I was convinced that we had a perfect little girl.

Now we had three-year-old Ronnie and our baby girl. She was born on Thanksgiving Day at the Portland Sanitarium. Ken couldn't wait to rush back to Aunt Mamie's house in Meadow Glade, where the family was gathered. He dashed in with the news, "It's a girl!"

She was three months old when another change began to take shape in our lives. We had never planned to stay with the store, but the success of the venture began to give Ken some second thoughts. For once we didn't have a money problem. We had a good car. I could go to Portland shopping when I wanted to. It seemed that Ken had inherited his grandfather's talent for business. He had people working in the store so could be gone when needed.

Without saying anything to me about the two possibilities before us, staying with the store or going back into the ministry, Ken felt that he needed to get away where he could think things through.

In the intervening years, Quentin had been drafted and served his term overseas. He was the supplier for the 43rd General Hospital, with the final months in France. It was a great day for our family when he called to tell us that he was back on US soil. He came to visit us and he and Ken began to talk of their old days up in the Valsetz woods.

"What are your plans now?" Ken asked him.

"I'm not sure," Quentin replied. "I've decided to take medicine. I guess the first thing is to get a job. It would be fun to get back into some outdoor work for awhile."

"You mean, like falling trees and cutting wood?" Ken asked, partly in fun.

"Hey! That wouldn't be a bad idea! I could get an old army truck. Where could we go?" The idea began to gel and they heard of a place up in the mountains east of Silverton, Oregon, where trees were available. Quentin found an Army truck at a good price, and they even found an empty house by a stream in that area.

I never really liked to live right by the store where Ronnie didn't have a play yard. I loved the woods and it wasn't hard to convince me to move for a few weeks or months. Ken would go back and forth periodically to take care of things at the store. He asked his cousin, Wendell, to be the manager.

The house was old but comfortable in a way, and I loved hearing the stream nearby. It was close to Salem, and Mom told me, "Send your washings home. I'll do them in the machine." Those weeks in the woods were a boon to our whole family.

After a few months, as winter was coming on, Ken came in the house one day to talk to me. "You know, it has done me so much good to be out working in the woods again. It seems that is where I always feel closest to God. Business is appealing to me, and it is nice to be out from under financial pressure, but I want to be sure that we are where God wants us to be. In the next few months we will need to make a decision."

I was happy to hear that from my husband. I had been praying earnestly for God's leading, too. With the wood venture over and back at our home by the store, we continued to mull the question over and over. "What should our next move be?"

We had been told to let the Union leaders know when we were ready to come back. Ken had been getting our financial affairs in order, the debts were all paid, and we would have a car paid for.

Finally, one day as we were driving to Longview to visit his parents, he asked me a vital question. "I seem to have some talent for business. We are doing well and could expand. I could be an active layman right here, and we could have a nice home in the country. What do you think we should do?"

Waiting for a moment, I just looked at him and said, "It would be nice to live comfortably and I'm sure you would do well. But if you really want to know, I would rather live in a tent and be a pastor's wife, seeing you preach the gospel."

It wasn't long before we received an invitation to go to Wenatchee to be the Associate Pastor with Elder Wilcox, a returned missionary from South America.

Chapter 50

Back On Target

Again we found ourselves driving to a new district, this time in Wenatchee, Washington. We were happy to be going back to our original dream. Our two precious children with us, and the conference truck bringing our furniture, we felt that this time we would be entering into the rest of our lives, wherever God should lead.

Driving through the mountains, we reveled in the beauty of deep woods, sparkling streams, and rugged mountain peaks. There was plenty of time for conversation. We talked of the disappointments, but also of the happy memories of our first year in the ministry. The Trudes would forever be our friends. That summer in the sawdust tent meeting was an experience we would never forget. The two years in the store gave us the financial push that we needed.

Looking in Ken's direction I spoke from my heart, "I am so happy to be going back. God has been so good and patient with us. I know you have a lot of financial ability, and you pulled that store out of the doldrums. I guess God could have blessed us to be good laymen, but I am convinced that He is leading us to go back to our original dream. You will be Pastor Fleck. I don't know where He will lead us, but I feel so sure that God is leading us to be workers for Him."

"Well, my dearest, I feel the same way. I guess the idea of being a successful businessman was appealing, but I, too, want to be where God leads us. I am so fortunate to have a wife who is willing to go with me, no matter what. You are an inspiration, and I know you will be the best pastor's wife you know how to be."

I smiled at him, with tears in my eyes. "You know, I have been praying every day that God would show us what to do. I still remember what I vowed at our wedding, 'Whither thou goest I will go.' And I am so glad that I will have the wonderful honor to be a pastor's wife. You know it was one of my childhood dreams."

Elder and Mrs. Wilcox, Harry and Belle, gave us a warm welcome. Ken told me later, "I feel that Elder Wilcox is a real Christian. It will be a pleasure to work under him. You know he was a Union President during their years of mission service in South America."

"Yes, his wife told me about that. They must be about ready for retirement, but we will be able to learn a lot from them. Maybe we might even be missionaries sometime."

Finding an apartment or house that fit our budget wasn't easy. Finally, one of the church members told us, "We have a prune shed we aren't using. There is a bathroom, of sorts, and I think we could fix up a little kitchen. If you want to arrange some living quarters in it, you are welcome."

So our first home in Wenatchee was in a prune shed! Since housing that needed help always challenged me, I found it fun to make the prune shed cozy for our family. The children would have plenty of room to play in the prune orchard! In a large central area of the shed we arranged our living quarters. We curtained off the bedroom area, found some used rugs for the rustic, wood floor, and by the time our few pieces of furniture were arranged we were home! I didn't realize that fixing up the prune shed would help to prepare me for the rigors of mission life later on.

It wasn't long until Elder Wilcox announced that he wanted to hold some meetings in Cashmere, about half way to Leavenworth. We found a house in Monitor, a small community just south of Cashmere. It was the parsonage of the community church. They would give us free rent if Ken would build the fire in the church every Sunday morning. It was a comfortable, older house with three bedrooms. The church and parsonage were in a small island where two roads met. It didn't give much room for the children to play, but at least we had a real house.

Ken and Elder Wilcox found a grange hall on a street near the edge of town that led up a mountain road, called "the Gulch." They discovered that a lot of people lived up that road. Elder Wilcox came up with a bright idea. "Let's buy an old school bus and you can drive up the gulch picking up the people to bring to meeting." That is what they did.

LaBreta wanted to come and stay with us that winter and go to the church school in Wenatchee. She rode a bus into town each day and then baby-sat our children. The meetings were a success. The large grange hall was well filled each night. Ken drove the bus, got the hall ready, led the music and provided the special music. My role was to play the piano and draw a chalk picture each night while Ken played the piano and sang. Mrs. Miller, my art teacher at Walla Walla, had provided me with enough ideas for pictures to last through the meetings.

One night it was snowing. Ken had taken the bus early to go pick up the people, and I came with the car. The front door was on the side of the building with half of the chairs in front and the others in the back, so I had to walk between and across to the other side and on up to the piano. I had forgotten something in the car and, at the last minute went hurrying out to get it, walking in shoes with high heels. I didn't realize that snow had stuck to my shoes. When I came in to the well-filled building and started across to the other side, that dance floor of the grange hall and the snow on my shoes sent me on a slide. I tried desperately to catch my self, but to no avail. After doing a little dance of my own out there, I finally went down! Only my pride was hurt, but it was one of my most embarrassing moments!

The district reached to Leavenworth, We had the services wherever Elder Wilcox sent us. Another young couple preceded us there. The young man, just out of school, apparently had a different concept than we did about his relationship with the senior pastor. It wasn't long before we began to get some strange stories. One of the local elders told Ken that he understood how hard it must be to work for an older man like Wilcox, and that we could be sure he would support us, even if Wilcox didn't approve. Ken sensed the negative influence of the young worker.

Ken was shocked. "You know, Brother _____, I am working under Elder Wilcox and I have found him to be an experienced and spiritual man. You need to know that I will always support him."

It was the last we heard of negative talk about Elder Wilcox, and that local elder soon began to respect Ken and work well with him. When Ken told Elder Wilcox about that conversation, he laughed, "Well, that young intern has plenty of self confidence. I imagine if the committee would ask him to be the conference president he would just answer, 'Brethern, I believe you have made a wise choice!'"

The first Sabbath we spent in that church, a family invited us to dinner. They had several children and lived on a farm. They were new converts and thrilled with their new experience. We were surprised that the main things on the menu were a big kettle of beans, white bread and a large jar of jam. They explained that the former young intern had taught them his concept of healthful eating. The poor people hardly knew what to cook or eat, but they were sincere, and very hospitable.

One day the intern told Ken, "I don't go for all this talk about agonizing in prayer, to gain victory over temptation. Just relax in the Lord."

It wasn't too much of a shock when we heard later that in his next district he and his wife had exchanged spouses with another couple, and sadly, they soon left the church.

The parish house where we lived was comfortable, but had one big problem. It was near an orchard and the house was infested with mice. We tried everything to rid the house of those pests. One day Ken opened his desk drawer. He called me. "Alcyon, come here!"

He pointed to the drawer. There, in a handkerchief he had left, was a nest full of baby mice!

"Where is the mama?" I laughed.

Not knowing what to do with them, he walked to the bridge over the river near the house, and let the mice swim for it!

After a few months in the Wenatchee district Ken decided that we needed a new car. We decided on a Chevrolet.

Before opening our first checking account after getting married, Ken had explained to me, "My parents were both on their checking account, but I remember my dad always had a hard time balancing his account because Mom would forget to fill out the stub. I think it is better to just have one person sign. I'll always give you the money you need."

I didn't object. Actually, when I was growing up there wasn't enough money to even have a checking account.

But when Ken took me into the bank to co-sign on the car payment contract, I suggested, "Maybe if I know enough to sign this contract, I should be on the checking account!"

It had bothered me that sometimes I had to take something back at the grocery store if I didn't have enough cash.

Ken laughed and said, "O.K. You win. I think it is time you are on the account!"

We were thrilled with our new car and we thought that with careful budgeting we could make the payment of $55 a month. Our salary had been increased to $156 a month, plus auto and rent allowances.

Moving into a larger house with the need for more furniture as well as the needs of a growing family on a minister's salary demanded close budgeting. There was little room for anything extra. We needed a hot water heater and wondered how we could manage that.

We decided to price them out while shopping in Wenatchee one day. At Sears we found a sale on hot water heaters. More than that, an easy payment plan was offered. It seemed a logical move for something so necessary.

After signing up for the water heater, we wandered around the furniture department and saw some more drastic sales. "Ken, come over here," I called to him. "We don't have any furniture for our bedroom except the bed. Look at this set that includes the head and foot board, as well as a chest of drawers and dresser." I could picture it in our bedroom. "The price has been drastically cut and it is offered on an easy payment plan."

"And what do you think about this matching rug?" he asked me.

Ken liked it, too. He did some figuring and thought that the monthly payment of $33 for both the water heater and the bedroom furniture would be doable. Our hearts prevailed over our heads and we made the leap. However, the new payment plan, combined with the payments on our new Chevrolet demanded a budget that made even an extra $10 for anything else almost impossible.

I needed a new dress and we decided we would fit that into the budget and found some material I liked on sale. I had the new dress all cut out and the skirt sewed and ready to attach it to the top. Leaving it on the dining table while getting dinner, I didn't notice that Carolyn, two years old, had climbed up to investigate. When I got back to it in the afternoon, I was horrified to see that she had taken the scissors and cut a big swath diagonally clear across the front of the skirt. I burst into tears. When Ken came to see what had happened, he saw the mutilated skirt. "There's no more material," I wailed.

"Don't you think we could find more at the store?" he asked.

"I don't know, but there isn't money to buy more."

"Well, let's go to town and see if we can find more of the same material."

We did find more of the same yardage. Ken, in his pity for me, managed to find the money, and I finished the dress. Carolyn didn't realize what she was doing, but I don't think that offence was repeated!

One day a letter came from Elder C. Lester Bond, the conference president. "The conference committee has voted to send you to Colville, and you will be the pastor of that district. There are three churches and a group. You should make your plans to move as soon as the present pastor leaves. We will arrange to send the conference truck to move you."

Needless to say, for us it was earth-shaking news. Ken would now be the pastor of his own district.

Chapter 51

She Knew Ellen White

"There's a house in Colville for rent," Ken told me one day. "It is owned by a member of the church there. Would you like to go and see it?"

We had moved into the house the former pastor left in Chewelah, but it was not in the center of the district and it was too small. We had been hoping to find a bigger house in Colville.

"Tell me more about it," I responded.

"Well, I haven't seen it, but they said it has two stories, and is close to the center of town."

We were definitely interested, and went to see the house. I was thrilled. True, it was old, but it was a real house. There were three bedrooms and a bath on the second floor, and a large bedroom, living room, dining room, large kitchen and a bath on the first floor. You lifted up a trap door in the kitchen floor that led to a cellar. That is where we would put the wringer washer.

The owner assured us, "I know the kitchen isn't much but I plan to put in new cabinets, and a new floor." They had already painted and put on some wallpaper.

I loved the whole house and couldn't wait to move in. We would sleep upstairs and the downstairs bedroom would serve as guest room and Ken's study.

Soon after moving Ken began to hold meetings in an upstairs hall on Main Street .One of the first nights we were getting ready to start the song service, when I called to Ken. "You need to come and look. A young man is crawling up the stairs on his hands and knees!"

Clark Hoagland, paralyzed from the chest down, was making his way to the meeting. He was one of our first converts. He was an accountant and seemed to do everything anyone else did. He married a young woman from our district, and they became faithful church workers.

Ken was busy visiting interested families and giving Bible studies. The meetings were well attended, and we were installed in the church as the pastoral couple.

On the Sabbaths that Ken preached in Colville, he would preach in the afternoon in Northport. One Sabbath evening, after spending some time with our members, we were driving home, when I looked up at the sky and exclaimed. "Ken, the sky is full of fire and color. Look! It is beautiful."

"Oh, that's the Northern Lights! We used to see them sometimes when I was a boy on the wheat farm."

All the way home that night we watched the sky with its dancing lights.

On the Sabbaths we went to Chewelah we went over the mountain in the afternoon to Gifford where the members met in a hall. They were so friendly, inviting us to their homes and loading us down with produce from their gardens.

Our first Sabbath in the Colville church we met some very interesting parishioners. There were two elderly ladies who lived together. They were both widows and became a very important part of our lives. The eldest was Emily Campbell-Fay. We were thrilled to know that she had been Mrs. White's secretary in Australia and had typed the manuscript of *The Desire of Ages.*

Knowing these two old saints was one of the brightest spots in Ken's ministry. They had a house that would have been an antique lover's paradise. It was a typical grandma's house, simple but warm with the treasures from their lives. They both wore gold rimmed glasses with their hair done up on top or their heads, dressed like they had for many years, but elegant, befitting their heritage.

Emily's sister was Belle Graham, whose husband was a captain on the Pitcairn. They liked to invite us for Sabbath dinner and the children loved to go and see their quaint house. They were good cooks and always did everything in good taste. Both Emily and Belle loved their young minister. He sometimes took them to town to do their shopping or other errands.

After we had been in our new district for several months the conference announced a Spirit of Prophecy week. Ken asked Emily, "Would you be willing to let me interview you in church on Sabbath about your memories of Mrs. White?"

"Well now, Pastor," she answered with a smile, "if you think it would help someone, I would be glad to do it."

It was a life changing experience for me to hear that meeting. She not only answered his questions, but she told some human-interest stories that gave us a glimpse into the real Ellen White. At the end, he asked her, "Tell me, Mrs. Fay. Did you really believe in her as a prophet?"

"Oh, yes! You couldn't live around her and not believe that! She was the kindest, Christian lady you could ever hope to know."

At that service, Emily told experiences that I would never forget. During the following years as a pastor's wife, I often told that story of hearing Emily Fay talk about Ellen White.

Besides Emily and Belle, there was another elderly lady with a rich Adventist heritage, Ida Tripp-Budd. Her brother, George Tripp, was in that first group of missionaries sent to Africa. They were the real pioneers.

Kenneth and I had read the book, *On the Trail of Livingston*, to the children. To hear about those brave people from someone so close to them was exciting for us. George and his young son were among those of the group who died with the dreaded fever. Ida Budd proved to be one of our dearest friends.

Someone gave Kenneth a mask, really just dark glasses on a big nose with a black mustache. One morning he was displaying the mask to the merriment of the rest of the family. I thought of Emily and Belle and suggested, "You know Mrs. Fay always has a sparkle in her eye. I think she would enjoy a joke. She and Belle think so much of you and would be good sports. Why don't you go over and knock on their back door?"

"Hey! That's a good idea. I could offer to split wood for them for something to eat!" They had a woodshed in their back yard and burned wood in their antique parlor stove.

Ken put his jacket on wrong side out and found a dilapidated old hat. Donning the mask he went over to their house, went around to the back door and knocked. When Mrs. Fay opened and saw this "bum" standing there, she gave him a scrutinizing look over her little gold-rimmed glasses, and asked, "Can I help you?"

"I just wondered, lady, if you could spare a sandwich. I'd be glad to chop your wood."

"Well, I have plenty of wood right now, but, come on in." And she opened the screen door and ushered him in. "Just sit over there by the table while I fix you something," she told him, handing him a *Review and Herald* magazine. "You can read this while you wait."

Ken opened the magazine and pretended to be reading, watching her out of the corner of his eye. She opened the cupboard and brought down a plate, placing it on the table, and then put the silverware beside it, and started to pull some food out of the refrigerator and put a kettle on the stove. By then, Ken had put down the magazine and taken off the mask, just sitting there. His benefactor looked his direction over the glasses that were down on her nose. Then, she took another quick look and exclaimed, "Why, Pastor Fleck!" She came over to take him by the shoulders and gave him a good shaking.

There was nothing wrong with her sense of humor. "Listen, Pastor, Belle just stepped out but she will be back soon. You have to do this to her!"

So Ken went back to the wood shed and when Belle came the whole scene was repeated, and she had the same exact response as her sister. They never tired in telling the story about their young pastor, and they just loved him all the more.

But we learned to know Emily Fay on another level. She was on the church board, and Ken could count on her to come up with wise counsel. There was another Senior Citizen, who was the head elder. Brother Maxon was a tall, stately man, and Ken appreciated him as a leader. Although he and Mrs. Fay were friends, they didn't always agree, and little diminutive Mrs. Fay and big, tall Bro. Maxon both knew how to uphold their views of things to Ken's secret amusement.

It was a busy time during the evangelistic meetings that we held. There was another one of our elderly members, Mrs. Page, who was very different. She was a quiet, stately person, always faithful in church activities with her presence, but we hadn't learned to know her very well.

One day she told me, "You know I just live around the corner from you in those apartments. I know that you are busy playing and helping with the meetings. It is hard to take your children. I would be happy to come and stay with them when you need to go out in the evenings."

"That is so generous of you, Sister Page. It is true that it isn't easy to keep them up and watch them at the meetings. Are you sure you want to do that?"

"Yes, I really mean it. Just put them to bed before you leave." Mrs. Page couldn't know how relieved I was. The meetings were five nights a week.

Besides helping my husband to prepare slides every day for the meeting that evening, there was cooking, cleaning, washing and ironing. Ken would come home from visiting, eat his supper, and change his shirt for the meeting. One week, I ironed nine starched, white shirts, besides all the rest of the ironing.

One evening when Mrs. Page came over to stay she suggested, "Why don't you leave your darning for me? I need something to do while I sit here and watch the children." In those days socks were darned until there wasn't room for any more holes. Each night when we came home I found a neat pile of socks all mended and back in the basket. If I happened to leave in a hurry without washing the dishes, I would find them all washed and put away. And that dear old lady would never take a penny.

One Sabbath we had company for dinner, and then in the evening a group of church members came over, and we served them some sandwiches, too. I hadn't had time to even wash the dishes from dinner. Busy in the living room with all our company I didn't notice when Mrs. Page stole in the back door. Before I discovered her she had all the dishes washed and the kitchen in perfect order.

When we first walked into the Colville church in our new district, I commented, "It looks like we have a lot of older members in this church. I wonder how things will go." We needn't have worried. Our Colville church was one we would never forget. It was our first district, but one that knew how to love and respect their pastor and family. How we did love them in return!

Chapter 52

Snow Bound on Thanksgiving

Kenneth was planning another series of meetings in the southern part of our district. The conference sent another couple to help him in the meetings and in the district, Dalles and Blanche Dull. They had two boys, Melvin and Lloyd who were close in age to Ronnie and Carolyn. They would live in Chewelah.

It was November and the Thanksgiving holiday was coming up. "What would you think of inviting the Dulls to our place for Thanksgiving dinner?" Ken asked me one day. "They don't have family nearby either."

"I think it's a good idea. Ronnie and Carolyn will be happy to have some one to play with."

They were happy with the idea and Blanche asked me, "What do you want me to bring?"

Between us we made up a menu that promised to be a real feast.

Thanksgiving morning, I heard Ronnie call, "Here they are!"

Dalles carried in the boxes of food, and Blanche began unloading pies and other special dishes. This would be a real old-fashioned Thanksgiving. Somehow it seemed appropriate in our old fashioned house!

We had just surrounded the table and asked the blessing when Ken looked out the window. "Do you all realize that it is snowing?"

The children jumped up from the table and ran to the front window. "Look at the big flakes! It is really snowing hard." They were all talking at once.

As soon as the pie was served, the children hastily ate theirs and then ran for their warm coats, hats and gloves, because the snow was already piling up. But the four of us continued our conversation around the table, savoring the delicious pies that Blanche brought.

While she and I cleared the table and washed the dishes, the fellows went out to watch the children and to peg a few snowballs themselves. Soon the daylight was turning to darkness. We visited in the living room with the warmth of the crackling fire in the wood heater. Reluctantly the children came in with rosy cheeks and cold feet and hands.

Ken and Dalles went outside again to check the weather, but the snow was falling faster than ever. "We should be going home," Dalles observed, "But I don't know about how the roads will be."

"No, you shouldn't venture out in this," Ken told him. "Driving will be hazardous."

"But we didn't come prepared," Blanche objected. "We can't impose on you folks like that."

"Don 't worry!" I interjected. "It won't be any trouble for us. This is a big house. We can make room. This will be a night to remember. The night we got snow-bound!"

The next day, the storm let up sufficiently for the Dull family to drive back to Chewelah. But that snowstorm was the beginning of a record winter. We never saw the ground again for three months. It was so cold, down to 38 degrees below zero one night, that we brought our frozen food home from the locker and left it on the back porch where it stayed frozen.

It was a white Christmas that year. Ronnie danced with joy when he found a new red sled under the tree. There were many good hills surrounding Colville that were ideal for sledding. On Saturday nights we had sledding parties. Some of the older members of the church would make a big bonfire on the side of the road and keep hot chocolate boiling, while we younger ones flew down the hills, then walked back up, pulling the sleds.

One memorable Saturday night there was a full moon. Ken told me, "You know there is a sledding party tonight on Knapp's hill. Do you want to go?"

"Have you checked the temperature?" I asked.

"Yes, it is 17 degrees below zero. We will need to put on all the warm clothes we have!"

"Sure, I want to go. Ronnie will love it, and Mrs. Page will probably be willing to stay with Carolyn."

We donned layers of clothes and joined all the younger set of the church out at Knapp's hill. They lived on a country road that was seldom used, and the hill had a long slope ideal for sledding. A huge bon fire lit the night about halfway up the hill. Sleds lined up and took their turn going down. It was quite a walk pulling the sleds back up.

Ken and I borrowed Ronnie's sled occasionally. And we would go down together, Ken on the bottom with his legs flying out behind the small sled, and me on top of him. With all that weight we really flew down the hill, and it seemed like we just kept going with the momentum.

But it was a romantic walk back up the hill pulling the sled. The full moon was so bright we could see all the surrounding area. "I've never seen anything more beautiful!" I panted. "This will be a night to remember forever!"

During those three months of winter with snow on the ground we learned to drive on slick roads. Ken had put sawdust tires on all four wheels. Most of our district was in hilly country, but the sawdust tires made driving reasonably safe.

One day Ken and I were returning from a Bible study in the mountains. There was a long hill leading down into the Colville valley. We had just started down that hill. The road was packed with snow, and there were mounds of snow on both sides from the snowplows. We hadn't seen any other cars and suddenly Ken pulled to one side and stopped.

"Ronnie's sled is in the trunk. I'm going to ride down this hill on the sled and you can follow me with the car."

"You aren't even dressed for sledding with that preacher overcoat and hat!" I remonstrated.

"It doesn't matter. This will be fun!"

I knew my husband as somewhat of a risk taker, and the stories from his childhood bore that out. But before I could say more he was out of the car and had the sled on the road. It was at least 5 miles down the hill. I clocked him at 35 miles an hour as I followed that ridiculous sight ahead of me, his overcoat flapping in the wind, and the sparks flying from the runners as he flew around corners.

When we reached the bottom and he was ready to take the wheel again, I chided, "Well, that's probably the first preacher that ever did that. Were you scared?"

"No, that was the biggest thrill I've had for awhile," he laughed.

"Well, it's a good thing we didn't meet any cars, and it is also probably a good thing that none of your parishioners saw you!"

"They would have enjoyed that," he insisted.

When the thermometer reached 38 degrees below zero, the pipes under the street froze and we didn't have any water until the street could be torn up to thaw them out. Maybe it was because I was born on the mountain in Canada during a snowstorm that, for me, it was the most beautiful winter of my life!

Chapter 53

Preacher's Kids

Ronnie was a lively six-year-old when we went to Colville. When Ken's mom and grandmother told me stories of his escapades as a child I knew we had a chip off of the old block. Even as a two year old I had to keep a close tab on him so that he wouldn't hurt himself by attempting too much or get into mischief. But he was a happy little boy who wanted to explore everything and try everything. Soon after moving to Colville he jumped into a swimming pool beyond his depth before he knew how to swim. It was fortunate for him that his father was close by. He seemed to know no fear.

Ronnie started school in the fall after he turned seven in May. We had a one teacher church school with a newly graduated teacher, Ora Lee Johnson.

That first day of school was exciting for him, but traumatic for us to see him march off to school with some other children who lived nearby. Ken had taken him to register the day before and he was raring to go.

He loved school and loved his teacher. Even though we had not taught him to read before, it wasn't long until he was bringing home his reader to show us how he could already read. Then, in a few weeks he could begin to read out of the Bible. By Christmas time his teacher came to us and said, "I would like your permission to put Ronnie in the second grade. He has already finished the first grade and is showing signs of boredom. I need to keep him busy."

I told her, "If you are sure this is the right thing to do, I guess you can, but I don't believe in pushing children in school."

Ora Lee assured me, "I won't be pushing him. He is eager to learn and finishes his work quickly." So Ronnie went into the second grade and was soon reading the Bible easily.

But his extrovert personality and eagerness in everything he did sometimes got him in trouble. It was a big shock to us when one of the church deacons, and father of another student, came to Ken and asked to talk privately.

"I think I need to tell you, Pastor Fleck, that your little boy, Ronnie, is stealing out of the Safeway Supermarket on his way to school."

When the man left, Ken came to me in the kitchen to tell me the dreadful report. At first I acted like a defensive mother. "I don't believe it. If they said he is stealing candy, it can't be true. He never eats candy, even when given to him. He always brings it to me."

It was true that Ronnie didn't eat candy. When he was small he developed a problem with asthma and we learned that sugar seemed to bring on those attacks. He had learned to leave candy alone and did not even seem to care for it.

But Ken quickly told me, "Don't be too sure about this. We need to look into it. When he comes home today I'll talk to him."

I was sure he would discover it was a mistake. But to my great chagrin, when Ronnie was confronted, he readily confessed that it was true.

"Why did you do it?" his father asked him.

"Well, there were some other kids there and they dared me to. They said they were sure I couldn't do it without being caught."

"And what did you do with the candy?" Ken asked him.

"I gave it to them. They wanted it."

"Did you know you were stealing?" his father countered.

Hanging his head, the little fellow agreed, "Yes, I knew."

His father talked to him about the seriousness of being a thief. Then they knelt down to pray and asked Jesus to forgive him and help him to never take anything again that wasn't his.

"Now, Ronnie, we have to make this right. You have some money from your allowance, don't you?"

"Yes, Daddy. I do. I don't know if there is enough."

After trying to remember how much candy he took, father and son walked up hand in hand the two blocks to Safeways and asked to see the manager. Ken knew the man personally and it was embarrassing to him, but he knew that Ronnie had to have this lesson.

When they went into the office, Ken said, "This is Ronnie, my son, and he wants to talk to you."

"Well, Sonny, what can I help you with?"

"Sir, I took some candy out of your store and I want to ask you to forgive me, and I want to pay you for it."

The manager was understanding and leaned down to respond. "I'm glad to know you are sorry, Ronnie. I'm sure you will never do that again. Thank you for being a brave boy and coming to me."

Talking about it later, I told Ken. "I couldn't believe he would do it, but I'm glad we found out about it" Still smarting about the situation, I continued, "It was pretty low of those kids to get him in trouble so they could have candy and then tell on him!"

"It may have been, but we can be thankful he has learned this lesson now. I don't think he will steal again."

When Ken was still single he knew a family with a beautiful little blue-eyed girl with curls. "Someday I would like to have a little girl like her," he thought.

Carolyn was that little girl, and she was her daddy's pride and joy. And she was the fulfillment of my dream of a little girl. She wasn't lively like her brother, but could amuse herself by the hour with simple toys. But her day to embarrass her parents came, too.

Our conference president, Elder Bond, and his wife often came to visit our district and occupied the guest room in our house. They treated us like their children. One weekend when they were there, Carolyn went into their bedroom and found Mrs. Bond's purse. Carolyn loved to get into my purses, not to take anything out but just to look in it. She evidently left it in a different condition than when she found it, and the Bonds told us about it. Needless to say, we were chagrined, and Carolyn had to be dealt with.

Ronnie still had some lessons to learn and we were forced to admit that our children were not perfect.

Another visit from a church member alerted us to the fact that the group of children walking to and from school was getting into other mischief. A basement window had been broken in a house by children throwing rocks. When Ronnie came home, again he was called into his father's study.

"Ronnie, is there something you need to tell Daddy about that you did?"

Ken had always taught the children that the truth was important. A lie could be worse than the deed itself. Ronnie didn't know what his father had heard, but he obviously had a guilty conscience. He thought a moment, "Are you talking about the window I broke in that church?"

Ken hadn't heard about that yet. "Is there anything else, son?"

"Well, yes, we threw rocks at a house close by too, and broke a window."

"What did you do?"

"We ran away." The whole truth was out.

So father and son had to visit the house and the church to make amends. Whenever Ken asked the children what the Bible says about sin, they would quote, "It says, 'Be sure your sin will find you out.' " It was a verse they never forgot.

Ken and I were beginning to understand something about the term, "preacher's kids." Other people's kids could do some of the same things and no one would think much of it. But our children needed to learn that "preacher's kids" are not privileged when it comes to doing wrong things. Ken and I were learning the same lessons that other parents had to learn. Satan would put all kinds of temptations before our children, and only with God's help could we bring them up to serve and love Him.

Chapter 54

Living With a Budget

We had been making the payments that pinched our budget for more than a year. Over and over again we discussed some need we had, and Ken would usually say, "You know there isn't room to spend money for anything we don't have to have. By the end of this year we should be out of debt and have everything paid for, including the car. We'll just have to tighten the belt for awhile yet."

One day I told Ken, "You know I have done aid work in hospitals. Remember my job at Paradise Valley? Why don't I see if I can get a part time job? Now that Ronnie is in school, I could work in the mornings while you study and watch Carolyn."

"I don't really like the idea," he replied, "but maybe we could try it for a little while."

I went to the Catholic hospital, walking distance from our house, and applied. The head nun was friendly and interested in me. So I went to work after buying a couple of uniforms and white shoes and stockings. The nurses on my floor were friendly and helpful, and we worked things out at home to try to make the plan work.

I enjoy people, and had even thought I would take nursing at one point in my life. My former experience helped. One day Sr. Humilitus, the supervisor, asked me if I would be willing to take a night shift in the OB section. I would be alone on the floor, but a nurse from first floor would be available when I needed help. We worked the new shift out with our situation at home.

For a time everything went well. I even assisted in deliveries. One night there was a delivery in the middle of the night. The nurse called the doctor and everything seemed normal. I was the one to prepare and put the new baby in the nursery. The mother went to her room and the doctor and nurse left. I was alone again on the floor. I kept looking at the new baby, who was sleeping peacefully. I was at the desk doing some charting when I suddenly had the urgent feeling to check on the baby again. She was still asleep, and I pulled down the blanket covering her, which no one had warned me to do, and there was blood under her. I pushed the button for the nurse downstairs and she came running.

When she saw the blood, she began to curse. "That ——— doctor doesn't ever tie the cord right." She called him, and he just told her what to do.

In the morning, Sr. Humilitus told me what a dangerous thing that was and that I should always uncover the babies to check on them. As a result that baby needed to stay in the hospital a little longer. I don't think the parents ever realized how close they came to losing her.

I went on working, but the scare took the heart out of me. I realized I wasn't trained for so much responsibility. I was unable to sleep for worrying that some other emergency could happen.

When Ken saw that I was so emotionally distraught he said, "I don't think you should try to work anymore. We can make it now."

So, after telling Sr. Humilitus that I couldn't keep on, she found a replacement, and I could again be just the pastor's wife and mother to our children. However, I knew I needed to give God the credit for giving me the impulse to double-check that precious baby.

Nurse-aids didn't make a lot, but my little salary helped to ease the budget for a while, and I could even go and buy a new iron!

One day Ken was working on the family finances, when he announced, "Do you realize that we just have one more payment on the furniture and two more on the car? We will soon be out of debt."

"That will be a wonderful day! We'll need to celebrate. And I, for one, vote that, from now on we only buy what we can pay for."

It would be our family policy from then on. The only exceptions would be for a car or house payment, and it wasn't long before we even paid cash for our cars, always finding a late model with low mileage.

After the first winter there, we had resolved a major problem. Heating the house with an oil heater with registers through the ceiling to heat the upstairs was not adequate. We realized that we needed to do something different. Oil was expensive and the house was not insulated well.

Ken talked to one of our members, Ora Laing. He was one of those people that knew how to do a lot of things. He told Ken, "You know, there is a place up in the hills where you can cut down your own trees and cut up the wood for winter. That is what I do. If you would like to, you can go with me this year, and I'll help you."

Sure enough, Ora did help him. They cut down the trees and used horses to drag the trees to where they cut them up for firewood. After a few Sundays in the woods, they had the old woodshed in our back yard full of wood, plenty for the winter. We took out the oil heater and replaced it with a cast iron circulating wood heater.

When it was all finished, Ken took me out to see the shed, filled to the rafters with wood, "I don't think we will be cold this winter! And it will cost us almost nothing."

"I'm so glad you did all this," I told him. "This should help our budget a lot."

The next winter, that proved to be the coldest winter in years, we were cozy warm in our house. The heater held the heat a long time. Ken would stoke it at night and there would be live coals in the morning. It was a sound I would always remember, Ken stomping the snow off his boots as he came in to load the wood box.

We hadn't been in our district long before we had been in the homes of most of our members and knew that many of them would be life-long friends. We loved the mountainous area, and we loved our old house. Little by little we accumulated the things that made it really feel like home.

There had been no intimation of any plans for ordination when Ken received a letter from Elder Bond. "The conference committee has voted that you be a candidate for ordination this year at campmeeting." The letter went on with other information regarding our district.

Ken finished reading the letter and then just stood looking at me with a big smile. We had not been concerned about when he might be ordained. We felt that God would be the one to set the time for that. "I am thrilled, Ken. I believe you are ready for this. I know your dedication and your sincerity. It is a solemn thought to know that God is ready to set you apart as an ordained minister. Did the letter say it would be at campmeeting?"

"Yes, it says that right here," he answered, referring back to the letter. "Evidently they will give us more details later."

Chapter 55

Ordination

We went as usual to campmeeting that was held at Walla Walla College. Our family, along with other ministerial families, was housed at the old West Hall. All of the workers were asked to be on hand several days early to help prepare for the meetings.

Ken came back to our room one morning with the news, "We have an appointment this afternoon to meet with the ordination committee. Elder L.K.Dickson from the General Conference will be there, as well as some of the conference officials. They will be talking to both you and me."

I wondered what they would be asking me. Actually, it was a friendly, but serious conversation. They did ask me about my attitude toward my role as a minister's wife. Ken was asked about his attitudes toward the ministry, the Adventist doctrines, and his personal relationship with God as well as about his loyalty to the remnant church. They gave us a chance to ask questions, and then gave counsel.

One question that Elder Dickson asked Ken was, "What would you do if the economy took such a turn as to take away all the salaries?"

"That is a difficult question," Ken replied, "but I think I would be constrained to still preach and carry on my work, even if I had to sustain myself."

There were encouraging words of "God bless you, Brother and Sister Fleck, as you dedicate yourselves to ministering to God's church." The interview ended with prayer.

On Sabbath afternoon, there was a special service for the ordination of several young ministers, including Ken. The wives were seated in the front row of the audience. I was seated beside Ray Turner's wife. They were under appointment to the mission field.

Ken's mom and Dad, as well as his Grandma Lashier were in the audience, and Ronnie and Carolyn sat with them. This was a high day for them as well as for us. We could never know the prayers that had ascended from his parents for Ken during his growing up years and especially those critical decision years of his youth.

As I sat there listening to every word my heart was thrilled beyond words. I felt that the ordination was for me as well as for my husband. We were and would always be a team dedicated to working for God. Again, in my heart echoed the words, "Whither thou goest, I will go," no matter where.

At one point that seemed especially significant and sacred to me, my eyes filled with tears. Afterwards one of the ministers came to me and said, "I was watching you, Sister Fleck, and I saw the tears in your eyes. They sparkled like jewels. God bless you, my dear!"

Chapter 56

Startling News

One day we were in Spokane and stopped in the conference office for a few minutes. When the treasurer saw us, he gave us some startling news; "You will be getting a letter from the General Conference soon."

Ken asked him, "What is that about?"

"Actually it will be a call to the mission field."

Surprised, Ken replied, "Really! Where is it to?"

Elder Perkins smiled, "I should probably let you wait to get your official letter, but I know how anxious you must be to know. It is to be the President of the Guatemalan Mission."

As we walked away Ken said, "Let's go into the waiting room for a few minutes. We need to talk!"

Finding a couple of chairs in a corner we sank into them. I spoke first. "Wow! That's pretty heavy news. Do you know where Guatemala is?"

"No, but I think it is somewhere in Central America. I think we need to go to a library and find out something about Guatemala."

There wasn't any discussion as to whether we would accept the call if it came. We had never asked for mission service, but we were both committed to going wherever God led us.

On the way home that day we couldn't think or talk of anything but the possibility of being missionaries. Ken was somewhat daunted by the idea of being a president of a mission. "I don't think I have any training for that," he admitted.

"Well, I'm sure the mission committee has decided that you have the qualifications to fit into that role. I don't have any doubt that you can do it!"

He laughed. "At least I have one good, loyal supporter who believes in me."

"Yes, you can be sure of that, but most important, my dear husband, we know that we can trust God with our future. If He asks you to do this, He will help you do it."

That evening at the supper table, Ken asked the children, "How would you like to be missionaries?"

Ronnie's eyes opened wide. "Are we going to be missionaries?"

"Well, it looks like we just may," Ken answered. "At the conference office today they told us that a call is on the way for us to go to Guatemala."

Carolyn, not yet five years old, had only heard us tell about missionaries, and had little idea of what that would involve.

That evening in worship, our topic was on missions, and we told them what we had learned. We knew the children would need preparation for such a change in their lives if we were to accept this call.

That same week when I brought in the mail I called, "Ken, I think there is a letter you will want to see!"

When I handed him the long envelope from the General Conference, he tore it open. "Well, here it is, " he said as he began to read. "Just like Elder Perkins said, it is to be the president of the Guatemalan Mission." He read the letter to me.

"I guess there is no question about accepting it, is there?" I asked.

"No, the call is pretty plain, and they do expect an answer. I think we need to pray about it first, but I don't have any reservations, do you?"

"No, I dreamed about being a missionary when I was a child, but I have to admit that I haven't thought about that possibility lately."

"Do you have any idea of all that this will entail?" Ken asked, looking me in the eye. "It says here that the term is for five years. I guess that means it will be five years before we come home again. Are you prepared for that?"

I looked right back into Ken's eyes. "Do you remember, my dearest husband, about what we vowed in our wedding? It was, 'Whither thou goest, I will go.' I haven't forgotten it, and I am just as serious now as I was then. You might add something to it. "Wherever God sends us I will go, and I can promise you that I will do my best. In fact, I am sure it will be the biggest thing that could happen to me."

Ken took me into his arms. "You can't know, my darling, how much I love you and appreciate the kind of a wife you are."

Snuggling into his arms I responded, "I am so proud to be your wife. I know that whatever God gives us to do, together with His help we will do it."

We were glad that Elder Perkins had prepared us for this dramatic turn in our lives. By now the children were excited about being missionaries, based on the little that we could tell them. But they sensed our excitement and knew this was something to look forward to.

Ronnie especially was full of questions. "When do we leave?"

I explained to both of the children that it would be awhile. "There will be a lot to do in preparation for this move. Remember when we moved here from Wenatchee? Well, this will be a lot bigger move than that."

Ken wrote the letter that would commit us to this new turn in our lives. We would be foreign missionaries.

In the days that followed there was more communication with the General Conference. There were documents and forms to fill out. First of all we would need physicals to be sure we were all healthy. The next letter assured us that we were now under appointment to go to Guatemala as soon as arrangements could be made. Among other things they would need to apply for permanent residence in that country for us. They didn't know how long that would take. But, in the meantime we should get the shots needed.

It was just before time for the General Conference Session in San Francisco. Another letter arrived. Ken came rushing into the kitchen, "Listen to this!"

"We would like for you to make arrangements to attend the General Conference session in San Francisco. You will be regular delegates under appointment to mission service in Guatemala."

"What do you think about that?" he exclaimed.

I was almost speechless. "Does that mean they will pay our way to General Conference?"

"I'm sure it does. That will be a first time for us at a General Conference, and I'm sure it will be a once in a lifetime experience. Just think, to go there as mission appointees!"

We spent the next hour discussing all the possibilities that faced us.

"Would we drive?" I wondered.

"They'll probably just give us a budget and let us decide that," Ken replied. "But, I would think it would be best to do that so we can take the children. This will be an experience that they will remember too."

Chapter 57

Under Appointment

In the end we did drive and Mom and Dad Logan came on the bus and met us there. We found a hotel a few blocks away from the auditorium where we could have two rooms together. It was very helpful to us as Mom was so good with the children. When we had to go to special meetings they kept them.

We were on time for the first evening meeting. We stopped at the registration booth and were given our nametags. We weren't sure where we were supposed to go, but we noticed that there were reserved signs indicating where delegates from each division would sit. We found our way to the Inter-American sign. We didn't know anyone, but someone spotted us and soon Elder Arthur Roth, the division president came, "You must be the Flecks. Welcome to Inter-America."

He began introducing us to others. The Wheelers were there, just returned from Guatemala where he had been a departmental director. Right away his wife, a friendly, out-going lady began to tell me all about Guatemala. "By the way, you will want to hire our maid. Her name is Maria, and she is a good, faithful girl."

I hadn't known I was supposed to have a maid!

Then we were introduced to a Guatemalan pastor, who was sent as an official delegate. He was Juan Castillo. His big friendly smile and enthusiastic welcome made us sure he would be one of our friends.

We met many others, those from Guatemala and also from other Central American countries, as well as the Union personnel from Costa Rica. We were seated among the rest of the group from Central America and soon felt like we were part of them.

We were happy to meet Elder N.R. Dunn from the General Conference and realized that he was one who had been communicating with us. His special area of work was with Inter-America. We didn't know it then, but these officials and workers would become our dear friends, and many of them would be staying at our house on their trips to our field.

At one point the Inter-American Division delegates were asked to meet after the meeting. We were told about the plans for when our division would be featured. We were to march up on the platform and to sing, "Mas alla del sol" (Far Beyond the Sun.)

Ken had studied Spanish in Academy, but I had studied French. Even so he didn't do too well, and I didn't know anything about Spanish. But we stumbled along the best we could, and it was a real thrill for us to be up there as part of them.

One morning a *Quiet Hour* employee found us. "We hear that you are missionaries under appointment."

"Yes, that is true," Ken answered.

"Well, Elder Tucker would like for you to be on a special television program featuring the General Conference session and the emphasis on missions. Could you meet us tomorrow morning?" And he told us the place and the hour. "We understand you have two children. We want them on the program too."

When we told the children about it, they were excited, and my folks were anxious to find out where they could go to watch it.

The next morning we were dressed the best we could and arrived at their studio on time. There was another young couple there who were under appointment to go to Japan. They were Paul and Barbara Nelson. We were taken to a make-up room where we were prepared to go before the cameras.

When Carolyn saw the girl apply the make-up to my face, she watched intently. When I was through, she looked up and said, "Do you think you are fancy, Mommy?"

I laughed and then bent down to explain why people have to do this to make them look natural on the cameras. I'm not sure she was convinced.

Meanwhile Mom and Dad Logan were looking desperately for a place to watch on TV. The time was getting close. Finally, they ended up in a bar, and were given two chairs in front of the TV!

The first Saturday night was the Inter-American program. We were up in front ready to go on the platform with all the rest of the delegates. It was a very impressive program, with a marimba band from Mexico in costume, thrilling reports from the different countries, and then at the end, our song, "Mas Alla del Sol." As we finished, Mexican girls in colorful costumes had baskets of flowers and went up and down the aisles, as well as from the front of the platform, throwing the flowers to the audience. It was a beautiful program and we were thrilled beyond words to be part of it.

During the rest of the session we met many new friends from that division. We spent quite a lot of time with Juan Castillo, asking him lots of questions about Guatemala. When we headed for home, we were full of the new experience of actually being missionaries and the reality came closer and closer. Now we would be going home to pack up our belongings and make the final preparations.

Chapter 58

We Have Arrived!

"Ken, the letter is here!" I brought the long envelope into his study. "This must be the letter they told us would be coming with all of the information we need."

Ken ripped the letter open and began to read. "This is it all right. This has the date to have our furniture ready to be shipped. It has some other information too. For instance, it will be a five-year term. We will have a month's vacation every year, but no allowance for a trip back home. Also there is an outfitting allowance."

We read the letter over a second time. "According to this, the truck will be here for our things in three weeks," I told Ken. "That means we really need to get on the ball. We'll have to do all our shopping before that so everything can be packed up."

When we wrote to our parents about this new venture in our lives, they had mixed emotions. First of all, being dedicated Christian parents, they were happy and proud that their children would be missionaries.

Finally, the day came when the conference truck arrived for our furniture. Walking out of the empty house for the last time gave me a lump in my throat. I had loved living there, and we had loved this, our first district. We didn't realize then how much we would look back to our time in Colville as our home back in the states.

The last Sunday in our district the Colville church had a farewell picnic for us. It was painful to tell our dear friends goodbye, especially the older members.

After all the goodbyes had been said, we were taken to Spokane where we boarded the train for the first leg of our long journey. We would spend time with both of our families while waiting for our permanent visas. That took longer than expected, but the children had time to get reacquainted with their grandparents and other family members.

Ken's parents, and Grandma Lashier, came to Salem to help my parents see us off on the train for New Orleans. From there we would have our first plane ride, a flight to Guatemala City.

"Are we really going to fly in a big plane?" Ronnie wanted to know.

But Carolyn wasn't so sure about that, "Will you be scared, Mommy? I think I will."

I understood her fears, "Well, it might be a little scary," I told her. "But we are going to Guatemala to work for Jesus. He will take care of us."

We arrived in New Orleans on a Friday and looked up a church to attend. It would be our last Sabbath in the US, before launching out on this new venture that would change our lives.

The next day, Sunday, December 10, 1950, we boarded Pan American Airways for Guatemala. I was nervous about the plane trip, but it went smoothly. The children were excited, especially when the stewardess let them pass out Chiclets.

Ken enjoyed the trip. At one time he had entertained the idea of being a pilot. But as we neared our destination, he became very serious.

Then as the loud speaker announced that we should prepare for landing, he was intently looking out the window. "Look, Alcyon, that must be the mountains of Guatemala. Yes, see that volcano!" Then shortly, he drew my attention again to the window. "We are flying over a city. Look at all the red-tiled roofs!" And then in a solemn note, "That is our parish down there!"

Nearly overcome with emotion, I just whispered back, "Whither Thou Goest..."

We'd love to have you download our catalog of
titles we publish at:

www.TEACHServices.com

or write or email us your thoughts,
reactions, or criticism about this
or any other book we publish at:

TEACH Services, Inc.
254 Donovan Road
Brushton, NY 12916

info@TEACHServices.com

or you may call us at:

518/358-3494